D1497961

FDR and the U.S. Navy

Edited by Edward J. Marolda

St. Martin's Press
New York

FDR and the U.S. Navy
Copyright © Edward J. Marolda, 1998. All rights reserved. Printed in the
United States of America. No part of this book may be used or reproduced
in any manner whatsoever without written permission except in the case
of brief quotations embodied in critical articles or reviews. For information, address St. Martin's Press, 175 Fifth Avenue, New York, N.Y. 10010.

ISBN 0-312-21157-0

Library of Congress Cataloging-in-Publication Data
FDR and the U.S. Navy / edited by Edward J. Marolda.
    p. cm. — (The Franklin and Eleanor Roosevelt Institute
series on diplomatic and economic history)
  Includes bibliographical references and index.
  ISBN 0-312-21157-0
  1. Roosevelt, Franklin D. (Franklin Delano), 1882-1945. 2. United
States—History, Naval—20th century. 3. United States—Politics
and government—1933-1945. 4. United States. Navy—History—20th
century. I. Marolda, Edward J. II. Series.
E807.F34 1988
973.917'092—dc21   98-3749
                                                                   CIP

Design by Acme Art, Inc.
First edition: August, 1998
10 9 8 7 6 5 4 3 2 1

Contents

Introduction

Franklin Delano Roosevelt's affinity for the U.S. Navy was of long standing; it dated at least from Christmas 1897, when the 15-year-old boy received a giftwrapped copy of Alfred Thayer Mahan's seminal work, *The Influence of Sea Power Upon History*. Inspired by the dramatic impact on the global stage of the new and powerful U.S. Fleet, often brandished by his illustrious cousin, Theodore Roosevelt, Franklin quite naturally focused his eyes on the sea. The young man's leadership, political, and administrative skills were tested and honed when he served as assistant secretary of the Navy under strong-willed Josephus Daniels during the First World War. That experience and FDR's psychological victory over paralysis in the years afterward helped steel the man for national and international leadership. As president during the 1930s, he endeavored with naval leaders, not always successfully, to build a combat-capable fleet and to deter the aggressor nations of Europe and Asia. One of Franklin Roosevelt's greatest achievements was his direction as commander in chief of the U.S. Navy and the other American armed forces during World War II, when the very survival of the nation was at stake.

In recognition of FDR's central place in modern American history and to commemorate Roosevelt History Month (officially designated by President William Clinton), on Tuesday, October 22, 1996, the Franklin and Eleanor Roosevelt Institute, the U.S. Navy Memorial Foundation, and the Naval Historical Center sponsored a conference entitled "Franklin D. Roosevelt and the U.S. Navy." The day-long event was held in the U.S. Navy Memorial's Naval Heritage Center at 701 Pennsylvania Avenue, Washington, D.C. The secretary of the Navy, the Honorable John H. Dalton, opened the conference by naming the next ship in the *Arleigh Burke* guided missile destroyer class as USS *Roosevelt* in honor of Franklin and Eleanor Roosevelt. Following this auspicious beginning and for the remainder of the day, scholars distinguished by their broad understanding of FDR's qualities as a statesman, politician, and wartime leader and the twentieth-century history of the U.S. Navy presented new interpretations of their subjects. Jack H. Watson, Jr., chief of staff to President Jimmy Carter, introduced the distinguished scholar, Professor Waldo Heinrichs, who delivered an insightful luncheon address. A reception sponsored by the Franklin and Eleanor Roosevelt Institute concluded the memorable conference.

Special thanks are due Mr. William J. vanden Heuvel, President, Franklin and Eleanor Roosevelt Institute, Rear Admiral Henry C. McKinney, USN (Ret.), President, U.S. Navy Memorial Foundation, and Dr. William S. Dudley, Director of Naval History, for their gracious sponsorship of this conference. Also deserving of thanks is Professor Douglas Brinkley, of the Eisenhower Center at the University of New Orleans, and Edward Prados of the U.S. Navy Memorial, who helped arrange for and prepare these proceedings for publication.

—Edward J. Marolda

ONE

NO TALENT FOR SUBORDINATION: FDR AND JOSEPHUS DANIELS

Kenneth S. Davis

I

DURING FRANKLIN ROOSEVELT'S YOUTH and young manhood, his great hero, upon whose public career he proposed to model his own, was his distant cousin and close family friend, Theodore Roosevelt. TR, you may remember, gained his first great national fame as a highly insubordinate assistant secretary of the Navy in the McKinley administration. Thus it was, with his eyes already on the White House, and with self-promoting insubordination already a viable option in his mind, that FDR, who had just been reelected to the New York State Assembly, accepted appointment as assistant secretary of the Navy in 1913.

He was then 30 years old, had been for 8 years married to TR's favorite niece, Eleanor Roosevelt, and was the father of three children. He had greatly impressed Josephus Daniels at the 1912 National Democratic Convention at Baltimore. Daniels, a key man in Wilson's 1912 election campaign, learned then that the young man loved the sea and was steeped in naval lore. Immediately upon

Daniels's selection as Navy secretary, therefore, Daniels asked the president-elect to name FDR his assistant. He was warned against this appointment by Elihu Root, who had been TR's secretary of state. "You know the Roosevelts, don't you?" said Root. "Whenever a Roosevelt rides, he wishes to ride in front." To which Daniels replied that a "chief who fears an assistant will outrank him is not fit to be chief."[1]

A couple of weeks after assuming his office, Daniels, while away from Washington for a couple of days, read in the newspapers what FDR had said to reporters upon becoming for the first time acting secretary of the Navy. "There's another Roosevelt on the job today," FDR had said with a wide grin. "You remember what happened the last time a Roosevelt occupied a similar position?"[2]

Actually, FDR was *not* really in a similar situation. For although Josephus Daniels seemed to most people a strange choice for the post he occupied (he certainly seemed so to FDR), he was no such vacillating mediocrity as TR's Navy superior had been. He was a North Carolina newspaperman, publisher of the *Raleigh News Observer,* aged 51 in 1913, a round-faced, blue-eyed, mild-mannered man, addicted to black string ties and pleated linen shirts, puritan in his morals, magnanimous in his human relations, and invincibly rural in his personal tastes, manners, and slow but sure habits of work. He stubbornly resisted efforts to rush him into decisions.

Like fellow cabinet member William Jennings Bryan, he was a pious Methodist, Prohibitionist, and pacifist at a time when pacifism was common among political Progressives. Like Bryan, he was a champion of the debtor class and a foe of "vested interests." He possessed no naval expertise whatever. He loathed all forms of aristocracy and flatly refused to recognize social-class distinctions between Navy officers and enlisted men. As secretary, he strove to democratize the Navy, opening the way for enlisted men to receive appointments to the Naval Academy and instituting an extensive basic education and technical training program for marines and sailors. His policies in general caused him to be cruelly ridiculed as an absurd country yokel by sophisticates, most of them with axes to grind.

Yet he possessed overall, according to one knowledgeable observer, "the exact combination of qualities needed to grapple with the Navy as it was in 1913."[3] A shrewd and adroit politician who realized how essential to executive success were persuasive dealings with Congress, adept at such dealings as his young assistant most emphatically was not at that time, he "entered the Department," according to our knowledgeable observer, "with a profound suspicion that whatever an Admiral told him was wrong and that every corporation with a capitalization of more than $100,000 was inherently evil." In nine cases out of ten his formula was correct: the Navy was packed at the top with dead wood, and with politics all the way through, and the steel, coal, and other big industries were accustomed to dealing with it on their own terms.[4]

Both the custom and the terms were abruptly changed.

As almost his first act after assuming office, Daniels advertised for bids for armor plate to be used in the construction of a new battleship, the *Arizona*. Only three American companies then made armor plate—U.S. Steel, Bethlehem Steel, and Midvale Steel—and these three submitted bids identical to the penny, $454 per ton. The secretary summoned the responsible company executives to his office and bluntly charged them with illegal collusion. They explained that Navy Department policy had long been to divide each armor plate purchase equally among the three companies at whichever bid was the lowest. Daniels replied that this cozy arrangement, no doubt dictated to a compliant department by the companies themselves, was now at an end. Bethlehem Steel, he pointed out, consistently sold armor plate to foreign governments at a price much lower than it charged the United States; in 1894, for instance, it had sold armor plate to Russia at $240 per ton while charging the United States Navy $616. He ordered the three companies to submit new bids. When they again submitted identical bids, he sent Roosevelt to New York City to consult with a British steel magnate who had just arrived there and who promptly submitted a bid so much lower than the three American firms had done that the latter were forced to drop their price substantially before the contract was awarded to one of them. Well over a million 1913 dollars were saved.

FDR then entered with enthusiasm into the campaign to save money for the Navy. Greatly aided by his own assistant, Louie Howe, he waged one successful battle after another against collusive bidding and monopolistic overpricing, and against the strong tendency of old-line Navy bureaucrats to condone if not connive in such practices. His motive for doing so, however, differed from Daniels's. His dominant concern was to build a U.S. Navy second to none. He saw economic efficiency as conducive to this end, economic waste as inimical to it. Daniels, on the other hand, opposed building a Navy any larger than needed for national defense, a need he measured much smaller than Roosevelt did, and he viewed his department's war against corporate greed as part of Wilson's New Freedom war for industrial democracy.

Nor did he, in his pursuit of New Freedom goals, shrink from measures his assistant deemed far too radical.

In the aftermath of the armor plate controversy, he pressed for construction of a government plant large enough to supply all the Navy's need for armor plate and shell casings. He skillfully piloted through Congress a bill authorizing such a plant, a bill Wilson promptly signed (the project was cancelled by the succeeding Republican administration before the plant could be completed). FDR opposed this project from the first. The most he favored was a small government plant that could be used to determine actual production costs, to experiment with armor plate improvement, and to serve "as a nucleus for great expansion in time of war." These three objects seemed to him "entirely legitimate" in that they did not contradict the basic premises of the private-profit system to which he was then, and forever after, religiously committed.

II

Joined with the policy differences between FDR and his superior were widely divergent work habits and procedures. The young man constantly complained to his wife of his superior's "Southern" reluctance to expend energy, his habit of postponing decision. "J. D. is just too damned slow for words,"[5] ran a typical outburst to his wife. When others in the department came to him with the same complaint, he sometimes remarked to them, with a wink and significant grin, that Daniels would be out of town on such and such a day; he, FDR, would be acting secretary. On occasion he showed his exasperation directly to his chief. "Mr. Daniels," began one of his scrawled notes, "Do *please* get through two vital things *today*."[6]

Daniels seems never to have resented overtly these strictures upon him. He admitted he was slow, cautious, deliberate, and disinclined to take any long step until absolutely sure of the ground ahead. He recognized this as, in terms of the job to be done, a sometimes serious deficiency. He counted upon his young assistant to supply a balancing zeal. And for this assistant, his fatherly love never waned. It was as much out of concern for the young man's welfare as for his own that he firmly corrected on occasion Rooseveltian acts inconsistent with his own administration policy.

There were two instances during Roosevelt's first year and a half in Washington when the United States was in some danger of full-scale war. In May 1913, the California legislature adopted a law prohibiting Japanese ownership of land in that state. Insulted and infuriated, Tokyo protested to Washington, in diplomatic language unusually strong for 1913. War fever ensued in both Japan and the United States. In both countries, responsible government officials strove to prevent any act that might incite hostilities. One such act—the transfer to Manila of U.S. cruisers then in China's Yangtze River—was urgently recommended by the war-eager Joint Board of the Army and Navy. Wilson, upon

Daniels's prompting, rejected the recommendation and, when the board persisted in agitating for it, threatened to abolish the board. The controversy thereafter subsided. But from the first to the last of it young Roosevelt stood on the militants' side, let them know that he did so, and very reluctantly adhered in his public statements to administration policy.

He was less circumspect in his public statements during a crisis in U.S. relations with revolutionary Mexico—a crisis with deep and tangled roots—that became acute in April 1914. Late in that month, when FDR was on an inspection tour of Navy installations on the West Coast, actual fighting broke out between American marines and Mexican troops at Veracruz. By then, FDR had publicly expressed his belief that war was inevitable. At the Bremerton base on Puget Sound, he had helped expedite the southward movement of Navy units. He now wired Washington for information concerning Navy plans for action on the west coast of Mexico. It was clear he wanted to be perceived by the public as the organizer of such action. Instead of the information he asked for, he received a request from Daniels that he return at once to the capital. He was on the train back when the United States and Mexico accepted an offer from Argentina, Brazil, and Chile to mediate the quarrel. Yet when a Minneapolis reporter asked him on the evening of April 25 what the crisis meant, he replied unequivocally, "War! And we're ready!" In Milwaukee the next morning he told reporters that "sooner or later . . . the United States must . . . clean up the Mexican political mess" and that the best time to do it was now.[7] In Chicago a few hours later he spoke of a "war spirit . . . sweeping the West like a prairie fire."[8] It was as if he could not bear to see closed the door he had opened to what he had heard as opportunity's knock.

When he arrived in Washington, FDR was at once closeted with his superior. Josephus Daniels gave him firm words of fatherly advice, impressing upon him the limits of an assistant secretary's authority.

III

Yet the tendency toward insubordination was increasingly manifested during the 31 months between the outbreak of World War I in August 1914 and U.S. entrance into that war.

To Daniels, as to most people of progressive mind all over the Western world, the outbreak of the war came as a numbing shock. He had not believed such a calamity possible in the twentieth century; he certainly had no clear conception of what the Navy's role should be. To Franklin Roosevelt, on the other hand, the war came as a great excitement and stimulus to action. A disciple of Alfred Thayer Mahan, he knew that the first thing to do was gather together the then widely dispersed U.S. Navy forces to create a fleet-in-being. He clearly saw other things the Navy must do to implement Wilson's immediately announced policy of strict neutrality. He promptly set about doing them. He became a dynamo of executive energy. "I am running the real work, although Josephus is here!" he wrote on August 5, 1914, to his wife, who remained at their vacation home on Campobello Island. "He is bewildered by it all, very sweet but very sad!"[9]

One may doubt that Daniels was quite as helpless as his assistant believed him to be. In retrospect it would appear that he was not abdicating his authority so much as passively delegating it, permitting it to be exercised by an assistant whose possession of superior knowledge in the technical and professional aspects of the Navy had been a reason for his selection. At any rate, this was the division of labor between the two men—young Roosevelt responsible for technical matters, Daniels for overall policy matters—which was then clearly defined for the first time and which continued through the remainder of Roosevelt's and Daniels's working relationship.

As regards national policy, however, the personal disagreement between the two was more profound during the period between August 1914 and April 1917 than it had been before.

Pacifistic Daniels remained fervently committed to Wilson's original strict-neutrality policy; he was convinced that U.S. entrance into the war would give giant corporations a control over the national economy fatal to true democracy. For this reason he opposed a rapid and huge preparedness program that, he was sure, conduced toward U.S. intervention. But Roosevelt was convinced that the United States must enter the war on the Allied side and, from the first, was one of Washington's most effective champions of preparedness. He joined forces with several of Daniels's bitterest personal enemies in active ways that would inevitably have led to his dismissal had not history moved in the direction he pointed.

After the United States entered the war, the area of disagreement between Roosevelt and his superior was of course much reduced. FDR, with his bold and imaginative initiatives, his immense zestful energy, and the invaluable assistance of Louie Howe, made major contributions to the national war effort. He dealt creatively with the Navy's construction program and labor relations, and was largely responsible for the laying, in the final months of the war, the great North Sea mine barrage. Daniels, though often dubious of his assistant's initiatives, fully appreciated the latter's value to the war effort.

IV

It was not until after the war ended, at a time when Franklin Roosevelt's private life was profoundly troubled, that his relationship with his superior was strained to the breaking point. As 1920 opened, Daniels came under vicious media attack by Admiral William S. Sims, prompting an investigation by a congressional committee dominated by Republicans, of the Democratic secretary's handling of his department. Long a troublemaker to the secretary, Sims, then president of the Naval War College at Newport, made so-called "sensational disclosures" of "the hopeless . . . maladministration, mistakes, and blunders into which the American Navy has fallen as a result of Mr. Daniels' policies."[10] Thanks to Daniels, ran Sims's major charges, the Navy Department, despite long forewarning, was woefully unprepared for war in April 1917 and had thereafter moved so slowly and inefficiently that the Navy was not on true war footing until six months after the declaration of war.

And FDR essentially corroborated those charges in a speech given at the Brooklyn Academy of Music on February 1, 1920. He said that the Navy had indeed been inadequately prepared in 1917 and that the department had been too slow and cautious at the top decision-making level. He himself had done all he could to speed things up. He clearly implied that his wholehearted commitment to the Allied cause and swift efficiency were in sharp contrast with the hesitancies, the doubting timidities, and the "idealistic nonsense" of both Daniels and Wilson. Even the forbearing Daniels deemed this speech traitorous. For the first and only time he seriously considered dismissing his assistant, crippling FDR's political career as a Democrat. He indicated as much in his diary. He probably would have done it had he not encountered in the White House at precisely that moment a personal enmity toward FDR so extreme that it provoked in him a defensive reaction.[11]

By then, Woodrow Wilson had suffered his paralyzing stroke. He was physically incapacitated and mentally disturbed. Insofar as the nation's supreme executive authority was being exercised at all it was through and by Wilson's wife. She—a foolish, highly emotional woman—told Daniels emphatically that she "hated" young Roosevelt, as did her husband, because he had publicly flaunted a warm friendship with British ambassador Sir Edward Grey after he knew that the latter had offended the White House in ways I need not describe. On the evening of the day of a White House visit, Daniels wrote cryptically in his diary: "FDR persona non grata with W. Better let speech pass."[12]

And so he did.

Personally, I'm convinced that this episode, coming as it did atop a pile of private troubles, was for the young FDR a defining moment. He was not much given to self-examination and not at all to self-revelation, then or later. He hid his deepest emotions and motivations behind a thick wall of what might be called loquacious reticence. But on this occasion he was appalled by what he had done, and was driven to assess his motives and measure his behavior against the standards of honor to which he was committed. Within hours after his speech he issued to the press an "explanation" of it that was essentially a retraction. In the following weeks, he repeatedly proclaimed, in public speech and private communication, his allegiance to Daniels and the administration, his pride in the Navy's record, and his contempt for those who sought to besmirch it. In a public statement that received a large press, he charged that the War College under Sims was turning out "holier-than-thou officers"—"gold-laced gentlemen" who aspired to run the Navy Department, using the civilian secretary as their puppet in dealings with the Congress and the public. Which, of course, was precisely Josephus Daniels's view of the matter. Always afterward, even when he was president of the United States and Daniels was his ambassador to Mexico, FDR addressed the latter as "chief," sought his advice, and often acted upon it.

As for Daniels, I think we all have reason to be grateful for the loving kindness and forbearance with which he dealt with a young man whom many others saw as brash, overly self-confident, and overly ambitious, but in whom he saw qualities destined to determine great and beneficent events in the history of the United States; indeed, in the history of the world.

NOTES

1. Kenneth S. Davis, *FDR: The Beckoning of Destiny, 1882–1928* (New York: G. P. Putnam's Sons, 1971), 320.
2. Ibid., 321.
3. Ibid., 323.
4. Ibid.
5. Ibid., 395.
6. Ibid.
7. Ibid., 338.
8. Ibid.
9. Ibid., 385.
10. Ibid., 592.
11. Ibid.
12. Quoted in Ibid., 593.

TWO

FDR AT WAR, 1913-1921

David F. Trask

SEVENTY-FIVE YEARS AGO Franklin D. Roosevelt came to Washington to become the assistant secretary of the Navy in the first administration of Woodrow Wilson, a post he held for the succeeding eight years. How did this early experience in government affect FDR's future activity, especially as president of the United States from 1933 to 1945? As late as the outset of FDR's first term, the columnist Walter Lippmann could argue with considerable plausibility that the man from the Hudson Valley was a perfectly estimable person with no discernible qualifications for the burdens of the presidency.[1] This judgment reflected the received wisdom of the day that great men did not become president.

Is it fair to maintain that FDR's achievements during the Great Depression of the thirties and the global war that followed in its train could not have been predicted on the basis of his previous career?

This question lends spice to examinations of FDR's activities in his several different guises before 1933, including his service as assistant secretary of the Navy. The details of this period have been covered extensively in many places, including the leading biographical works.[2] The English scholar Michael Simpson is soon to publish a thorough study of FDR in all his connections with the Navy. The objective here is to offer some generalizations on the *meaning* of FDR's service during World War I and its connection with the qualities of leadership that he manifested in his mature years.

FDR's designation as assistant secretary of the Navy in 1913 came about for one reason, and that was his name. He had no special qualifications for the position other than an interest in maritime affairs and yachting. His prior public service consisted of a stint as a state legislator in Albany. It conformed with the political interests of the Wilson administration to take on a relative of Theodore Roosevelt, particularly one from the state of New York. But this advantage had a dark side. FDR brought not only his name to Washington. There was always the possibility that he might become a loose cannon in the manner of Theodore Roosevelt, specifically when TR was assistant secretary of the Navy in President William McKinley's administration. FDR's evident choice of TR as a model lent cogency to this fear as did TR's rapid conversion into Wilson's leading political critic.

FDR enjoyed a certain standing in the Wilson administration, but he could not escape wariness on the part of some fellow Democrats. His task was to retain his Rooseveltian image without ruffling the feathers of the party leadership. He had to demonstrate uncommon loyalty to the Democratic Party and the stern Presbyterian at its head. Above all he had to retain the confidence of the secretary of the Navy, Josephus Daniels, a leader of the Bryanite faction in the Democratic Party who proved loyal to Wilson. Would FDR subordinate himself to the folksy North Carolina journalist who would soon become unpopular with many in the career naval service?

Following is a summary of FDR's activities as assistant secretary of the Navy.

He appears to have performed adequately as an administrator, concentrating on the affairs of the naval yards. In this role he gained first-hand knowledge of the ways in which strong central leadership could serve the national interest. Wilson's successful domestic reforms of 1913-1916 revealed the ability of government to help reorder the relationships between the basic elements of the polity to cope with dislocations stemming from the sweeping industrialization and urbanization of the country. The wrenching adjustment of the federal government to the demands of belligerency during 1917-1918 deepened his understanding that centralization could serve the nation well in moments of extreme crisis. The example of the wartime mobilization deeply influenced the national response to the Great Depression and global war, in great part because of FDR's experience during 1917-1918.

As assistant secretary, FDR identified to a degree with a dynamic, reform-minded element in the naval officer corps. This group, following the recommendations of the naval publicist Alfred Thayer Mahan, advocated construction of a great battle fleet capable of competing with those of the leading naval powers, including Great Britain, Germany, and Japan. The reformers soon found themselves at odds with Josephus Daniels, who effectively resisted efforts to expand the Navy inordinately and to weaken civilian control of the naval establishment. FDR placed himself in accordance with the Wilsonian recognition that the Navy was the first line of defense but also with the antimilitarist traditions of the United States, manifest especially in the outlook of Wilson's first secretary of state, William Jennings Bryan. When Wilson eventually came to support a navy second to none and then led the country into the First World War, advocates of a great navy suddenly found themselves with political support for naval expansion on an undreamed-of scale. This circumstance helped FDR to maintain his loyalty to the administration while consorting with the reformers who wanted to modernize and strengthen the Navy.

Like Theodore Roosevelt, FDR at times found himself uncomfortable in a civilian role during wartime, desiring a close tie to the front line. This aspiration found expression in 1918 when he was dispatched to Europe on a tour of inspection. Although he visited Britain, France, and Italy, and also the Western Front, nothing of significance stemmed from the trip. It ended sadly. FDR contracted influenza and was returned to the United States.

Of great interest is FDR's sustained support for close Anglo-American cooperation. During his European trip he interested himself in this matter but had little success, a byproduct of increasing tensions between London and Washington as the war approached its end. Some of the limitations imposed on FDR become apparent in this comment by First Lord of the Admiralty, Sir Eric Geddes, in a report to Prime Minister David Lloyd George on August 26, 1918: "Mr. Roosevelt, like all capable men, while his energy is much admired, is not without his own difficulties, and I am told that any agreement come to with him, or any agreement which he recommended as a result of a conference here, would start prejudiced."[3]

FDR's fortunes turned upward in 1920 when Governor James Cox, the Democratic candidate for the presidency in 1920, chose him as his running mate on the national ticket. Again FDR's name and his background in New York politics led to another emulation of TR's career, a run for the vice presidency. Cox, of course, was overwhelmed in the Republican landslide of 1920, but FDR gained considerably from it. His travels broadened his knowledge of the country and his acquaintanceships among the party leadership. He now enjoyed national standing.

And yet, a comparison of the FDR of 1913 with the FDR of 1921 does not suggest that he had acquired the inner resources--the strength of character, the moral courage--that are necessary to lead a great nation in moments of desperate crisis. The striking good looks and the gaiety of 1913 had endured, and national standing had been acquired, but there was little in his makeup in 1921 to suggest that he might some day become a great president.

To gain insight into FDR's acquisition of the inner resources that served him so well in later years, historians must turn to his harrowing experience during the years between 1921 and 1933. Two developments are of supreme importance:

One was FDR's struggle with infantile paralysis, which struck him soon after his unsuccessful run for the vice presidency. He might simply have accepted his illness and confinement to a wheelchair, giving up all thought of public life, but for a decade he struggled to regain the use of his legs. He spent lengthy periods in Florida and later at Warm Springs, Georgia, in search of a cure, but he was never able to walk again. Although his public life was necessarily limited while pursuing a cure for his paralysis, FDR made notable contributions to the development of facilities at Warms Springs designed to treat victims of poliomyelitis.

The second event of importance was FDR's return to active politics. In 1928 he felt able to resume national political activity, nominating Alfred E. Smith for the presidency at the Democratic National Convention. His appellation for Smith, the Happy Warrior, gained popularity. Although Smith was defeated, FDR was elected governor of the state of New York, rising to still another of TR's posts. Soon the crash of the New York Stock Exchange precipitated the Great Depression, and FDR was plunged into the work of dealing with it. The executive experience gained during his four years in Albany proved most useful after he entered the White House in 1933.

If students of the Roosevelt administration wish to identify the challenges that created the composure, the confidence, the energy, and the character that served FDR so well as chief executive, they must concentrate on the years between 1921 and 1932, and especially on the fight to overcome infantile paralysis, but this conclusion should not obscure the benefits that accrued to FDR during his first exposure to national government during World War I. What happened to him during the 1920s enabled him to make good use of the knowledge he gained during the First World War when he became president of the United States. The strength and competence that FDR exuded as he moved among the

American people with his pince-nez in place and his cigarette holder in hand stemmed from his extraordinary attempt to overcome a terrible personal tragedy. The good looks and the gaiety remained. His inner resources came to the surface when he was tested, not by war but by fate. His triumph took place not on a battlefield like the San Juan Heights but in the serene environs of Warm Springs, Georgia. It is fitting that FDR's life ended there in April 1945.

NOTES

1. Frank Freidel, *Franklin D. Roosevelt: A Rendezvous with Destiny* (Boston: Little Brown and Co., 1990), 68.
2. The principal sources for this paper are: David E. Cronon, ed., *The Cabinet Diaries of Josephus Daniels* (Lincoln, Ne.: Univ. of Nebraska Press, 1963); Freidel, *Franklin D. Roosevelt;* David F. Trask, *Captains & Cabinets: Anglo-American Naval Relations, 1917-1918* (Columbia, Mo.: Univ. of Missouri Press, 1972).
3. Quoted in Trask, *Captains & Cabinets,* 296.

THREE

JOSEPHUS DANIELS, FRANKLIN ROOSEVELT, AND THE REINVENTION OF THE NAVAL ENLISTED MAN

Ronald H. Spector

EARLY IN 1913, Mildred Dewey, wife of the hero of Manila Bay, wrote to her stepson about a visit by Navy Secretary Josephus Daniels and Franklin D. Roosevelt. "The secretary this morning brought his new assistant to call upon me and to see your father's treasures. Mr. Roosevelt is a very handsome young man . . . most charming and enthusiastic . . . I predict that if this young man lives, he is going far."[1]

Later biographers of FDR have largely agreed with Mrs. Dewey. They view Roosevelt's years as assistant secretary of the Navy under Daniels as an important episode in his apprenticeship, after which he was to go far. There is less agreement about the significance of Daniels's many years as head of the Navy Department, during most of which Roosevelt served as his junior partner.

Both Daniels, a canny former newspaper editor, and Roosevelt, ably assisted by Louis Howe, were adept at public relations and spin control long before these terms came into general use. These talents were best displayed in Daniels's two-volume memoirs, still treated as an important primary source. They portray a down-to-earth man of the people, ably abetted by his talented assistant, fighting to bring common sense, democracy, and honesty to the Navy.[2] This was the view taken by such observers as Ernest K. Lindley, who recalled that "Daniels entered the Navy department with the profound suspicion that whatever an admiral told him was wrong, and that every corporation with a capitalization of more than $100,000 was inherently evil."[3]

To many of his contemporaries, however, especially preparedness advocates, professional naval officers, and "big navy" enthusiasts, Daniels appeared to be little more than a well-intentioned country hick whose ill-considered dabbling in naval affairs reduced the efficiency and readiness of the service. Roosevelt himself wrote to his wife, "I am running the real work, though Josephus is here. He is bewildered by it all. Very sweet but very sad!"[4]

Naval officers were shocked and surprised at Daniels's appointment of a civilian professor to head the English Department at Annapolis and his order changing naval uniforms to eliminate the stiff choker collars. He infuriated them with his order banning beer and wine from the wardroom mess. His Aide for Operations, Rear Admiral Bradley Fiske, predicted that this ill-starred measure would drive officers to "the use of cocaine and other dangerous drugs."[5] (His prediction was accurate, though premature.)

Daniels's critics' view of him as a strong-willed, ill-informed bumbler who refused to heed the advice of the experts was well illustrated in a 1915 cartoon in *Life* that showed Daniels as a little boy playing enthusiastically but destructively with a range of nautical toys, while "nurse Columbia" advises him, "You Have Done Very Well, Josephus, But Don't You Think You'd Better Play With Something Else For Awhile?"[6] As for FDR, he is often portrayed as steering a tortuous course between his loyalty to

Daniels and his more sympathetic view and closer relationship with the line officers and "big navy" advocates.[7]

This chapter examines Daniels's and Roosevelt's ideas about the Navy's enlisted personnel problems in an era when such problems had become critically important. Those problems had much in common with those confronting the British Royal Navy and other navies in these same years. No one has ever suggested that Daniels's and Roosevelt's contemporaries at the admiralty, Admiral Sir John Fisher, First Sea Lord from 1904 to 1910, and Winston Churchill, First Lord from 1911 to 1915, were populist crusaders or anything other than thoroughly relentless modernizers.[8] Yet their approach to issues of personnel were similar—often identical—to those of Daniels and Roosevelt. Consequently Daniels cannot be understood either as a naive country bumbler or as a fearless crusader for democratic values but must be seen as fundamentally a modernizer.

If modernity is associated, as it usually is, with commitment to meritocracy, technical expertise, and education above claims of tradition, breeding, or family, Daniels can be considered more "modern" than most professional naval officers. Though surrounded by sophisticated weapons and mechanical devices, many line officers in the early years of the twentieth century were temperamentally, culturally, and psychologically ill-suited to make the organizational and personnel changes necessary to adapt to modern naval warfare.

In his studies of industrializing America, Herbert Gutman postulates a "working class culture" of preindustrial values, customs, and traditions attempting to resist the "modernizing" and rationalizing efforts of managers and employers.[9] Whether or not Gutman's ideas provide an accurate way of understanding the experiences of workers in industrial America, they do provide a useful way of approaching the experience of sailors in late-nineteenth- and early-twentieth-century navies, where in essence the situation was exactly reversed. Many naval officers of the 1880s and 1890s had an intense dislike for gunnery practice and other types of realistic battle drill because such exercises tended to spoil the paint and brasswork of their ships; conversely, they continued to advocate the supreme importance of sail training long after it had ceased to have much practical value.

Thus the "managers and employers" in the navies, that is, the officer corps, were almost invariably strongly wedded to preindustrial values, customs, and practices, while the sailors, especially those responsible for the operation of the engineering plant, gunnery, fire control, and communications, represented the new forces of science and industrialization. "It is only the popular imagination that pictures a blue jacket as always heaving a rope or tossing an oar," wrote a British journalist. "A pair of pliers is more use to him than an oar; he has much oftener a piece of paper than a rope in his grasp."[10] Even in the Russian navy at the turn of the century, recruits experienced in factory work, skilled trades, or clerical occupations composed about 60 percent of new inductees, compared to about 2 percent in the Russian army.[11]

In his history of naval enlisted men, Frederick S. Harrod observes that Daniels's annual reports "leave the impression that Daniels must have invented enlisted men."[12] This is in fact correct. Daniels and Roosevelt sensed that the U.S. Navy's enlisted force would have to be invented, or rather reinvented, to meet the needs of a new era of naval combat. The roles and status of industrial-age sailors had altered considerably from the days of sail. Sailors in machine-age navies were far more specialized and carried a greater weight of individual responsibility than in the age of sail. By the first decade of the twentieth century, all great navies had specialized schools ashore offering courses of up to a year in length for blacksmiths, engine-room technicians, gunners, torpedo men, cooks, armorers, electricians, paymasters, hospital men, and many others specialties. In 1906, the U.S. Navy had more than two dozen different specialized ratings and nine specialized schools. "I believe the time will shortly come when we will permit no man to serve in the Navy who has not had some little experience as a chauffer or as a machinist or as a mechanic or as an electrician or has not begun to learn some of the trades and vocational occupations needed in the Navy," Daniels told Congress.[13]

The secretary declared that "every ship should be a school," and issued a general order requiring two hours of instruction daily in general education and technical subjects for sailors in all ships and stations.[14] Daniels's reform received widespread praise in the press but many naval officers who were obliged to conduct the instruction were less enthusiastic. Nevertheless Daniels's idea of shipboard education, which by 1919 had evolved into a system of correspondence courses, became a permanent feature of twentieth-century navy life.

The most basic problem facing the modernizers in all navies in the first decade and a half of the twentieth century was simply finding men to man their rapidly expanding fleets. For the United States Navy even more than for the Royal Navy, rapid growth in the size and number of ships in commission meant a critical need for additional manpower. In 1896, two years before the Spanish-American War, the total authorized strength of the U.S. Navy was 10,000 men, only 1,800 more than it had been ten years before. By the turn of the century it had doubled to 20,000 men, and by the time Teddy Roosevelt's Great White Fleet began its voyage around the world, the Navy had almost 37,000 men. In 1914 it had over 51,000.

In the same years that it was doubling and tripling its size, the U.S. Navy also carried out a relentless ethnic and racial purge of the enlisted force. During the nineteenth century the U.S. Navy had recruited its sailors from among the traditional seafaring populations of coastal cities in the United States and abroad. In 1890 only 58 percent of the Navy's enlisted force were citizens and only 47 percent were native born. "What pride can an officer feel in his vain attempts to arouse some national spirit and esprit in such crews?"

lamented Commander William F. Fullam.[15] It is less than surprising that, given the rampant nativism and suspicion of immigrants held by many "old line" Americans at the turn of the century, naval officers should conclude that only white, native Americans would do. "We want boys who have never seen and do not know any other flag than the American, who have good American backgrounds, who have no Old World allegiances or affiliations. We want the brawn of Montana, the fire of the South, and the daring of the Pacific slope," declared Commander Francis H. Higginson, commandant of the Newport Naval Training Station.[16] As late as 1919, the Navy Department explained to a congressman who wished to know why recruiters never advertised in foreign-language periodicals published in the United States that "the boy from the farm is considered by the naval recruiting service to be the most desirable material." Foreign-language newspapers were most likely to be read by "men residing in the larger industrial cities."[17]

The U.S. Navy's efforts were remarkably successful. In 1899, 20 percent of the enlisted force were not citizens. In 1910, despite a 600 percent growth in the number of sailors, less than 2 percent were noncitizens and more than 88 percent were native-born Americans; this in a year in which 14 percent of Americans were foreign born.[18]

The Navy's program to eliminate African-Americans was equally successful, though considerably less publicized. There is good evidence that blacks constituted about 10 percent of all Navy enlistees in the 1880s and 1890s. By 1906 less than 1 in 30 sailors were black, and by 1930 there were less than 500 black sailors in a navy of 80,000 men. Long before this time the Navy had adopted an informal policy segregating blacks and assigning them only to menial jobs. As Daniels explained to a senator in 1917, "there is no legal discrimination shown against colored men in the Navy. As a matter of policy, however, and to avoid friction between the races, it has been customary to enlist colored men in the various ratings of mess man branch . . . and in the lower ratings of the fire room, thus permitting colored men to eat and sleep by themselves."[19]

The nativist, "whites only" Navy was expected to attract only "men from the best walks of life," in Daniels's words. Like the Royal Navy, the U.S. Navy established an ambitious and comprehensive recruiting system, one geared to presenting the twentieth-century bluejacket not as a rakish adventurer with a girl in every port but as a sort of well-traveled, high-tech boy scout. "Only men of sound mind and clean life are acceptable," Daniels wrote. "The Navy is no place for shiftless, purposeless men. No liquor is allowed aboard ships, no gambling and profanity is a violation of the regulations."[20] Daniels told Congress that "we have changed the style of our recruiting literature. We burned a bushel of literature which showed young men going into tropical climates and associating with women half-dressed (sic). These posters promised if a man enlisted into the navy or the marine corps he would have opportunities that appealed to the lowest. . . . Instead, every piece of literature that now goes forth says that the young man who now comes into the navy will have an opportunity to be educated."[21] Daniels and Roosevelt were especially annoyed at the practice of some judges of offering youthful offenders a choice between imprisonment and joining the Navy. "The Navy is not a reformatory," complained Roosevelt to the press in 1915.[22] Yet throughout the Wilson administration judges continued to sentence young men to years of character building in the sea service.

Despite the continued presence of these few youthful felons, however, the Navy was generally successful in finding the high-quality recruits it was seeking. Large numbers of young men were attracted by the possibility of foreign travel or the opportunity for technical training, or simply by boredom with civilian life and desire for adventure.[23] The state of the economy also had a marked impact on the number of applicants for enlistment. Recessions or localized spells of unemployment were powerful inducements to try the relatively stable and secure jobs offered by the Navy. From 1905 to 1914 the U.S. Navy accepted only about one in four men who applied for enlistment.[24]

Keeping the men proved a bigger problem. Unlike the Royal Navy, the U.S. Navy had no system of long-term enlistments. In 1910 over 74 percent of the total enlisted force had served less than four years—the length of one enlistment period. "Instead of congratulating ourselves that the 7800 vacancies which occurred during the last year were made good by recruit enlistment, we should rather deplore the loss of 25 percent of the enlisted force in one year," declared one naval officer in 1906.[25] A substantial number of men proved unwilling to wait the required four years before leaving the service. In the years between 1900 and 1908 the U.S. Navy lost an average of slightly more than 15 percent of its enlisted force each year to desertion.[26]

Daniels and Roosevelt concentrated on improving service conditions as a means of discouraging desertion and encouraging reenlistments. "I am the father of more than 50,000 young men," Daniels declared in a public address, "and there is nothing more upon my heart than to see men of strong Christian character living clean lives for home and kindred and country."[27] Daniels reduced the cost of uniforms, improved the quality of goods sold in ship stores, and reformed the naval disciplinary system so that sailors found guilty of serious infractions could be sent to disciplinary barracks and then returned to duty rather than sentenced to prison. All these measures paralleled or anticipated similar measures carried out by Fisher or Churchill in England.

Daniels also encouraged the installation of laundries aboard ship. By 1914, many Navy ships also had electric ice cream makers, a development applauded by paymaster George P. Byer, who believed that the Navy's "clear-eyed, intelligent American youths . . . know what clean living and good fare are, and they have the usual American notion of the festive nature of ice cream."[28] Aware of the appeal of the "join the Navy and see the world" slogan, Daniels also encouraged fleets and squadrons to make frequent visits to foreign ports.

Like Churchill, Daniels attempted to establish a program to allow outstanding enlisted men to attend the U.S. Naval Academy. Like Churchill, he met with indifferent success but established a precedent for the future. Both Fisher and Churchill wished to broaden the base of the officer corps by providing opportunities for enlisted men and others of modest means to enter the Royal Naval Colleges at Dartmouth and Osborne. The tuition at these colleges was equal to that of many of the best public schools; and unlike the public schools, the naval colleges offered no scholarships. Admiral Fisher estimated that there were about "1,500,000 people in the United Kingdom with incomes sufficient to pay the cost of officer training. Of the remaining 41,500,000 no single one can hope to become an officer in the Navy."[29] Churchill as First Lord of the Admiralty agreed that "we are drawing our Nelsons from too narrow a class." In 1912 he introduced a plan for commissioning a handful of enlisted sailors and marines. Yet even this modest program met with great opposition and few sailors ever achieved commissioned rank.[30]

Daniels was somewhat more successful. Though attendance at Annapolis was free and sons of poor families were sometimes appointed, Daniels feared that "ambitious youth who have no pull" would seldom be appointed.[31] In 1914 Daniels succeeded in persuading Congress to allow the secretary the authority to appoint 15 enlisted men to the Naval Academy each year. By 1918 the number had grown to 100 and in 1919 the Navy opened preparatory schools in Norfolk and San Diego to provide special courses to promising bluejackets preparing to take the Naval Academy entrance exam.[32]

In the end it is doubtful whether Daniels's and Roosevelt's efforts had any lasting impact on enlistment and retention rates. In 1913 and 1914, reenlistment rates were 57 percent and 65 percent, about what they had been during the previous five years. Retention rates did reach an all-time high of 72 percent during 1915 and 1916 but this was in a period of unprecedentedly high unemployment.

Peacetime retention rates never reached the 83 percent claimed by Daniels in his memoirs. With the end of World War I, reenlistment rates fell to 36 percent in 1919 and 1920.

The inescapable fact was that there remained a wide gap between the rhetoric about wholesome, clean-living, and educational navy life and the reality. On occasion letters providing a sailor's-eye view of life in the Navy and of its perceived hardships and injustices would reach influential congressmen, editors, clergymen, or educators. "If some state would only start a movement to compel naval officers to treat the enlisted men like human beings and not like dogs . . . that state would earn the thanks and gratitude of over 60,000 enlisted men," wrote one sailor in 1914 to his hometown paper.[33] "I have heard officers speak to boys in tones that chilled me," wrote Petty Officer Felix Shea, "not harsh words—just impersonal sneers without purpose or reason. . . . I have known boys to go ashore on Saturday morning without money and stay away until Monday morning without food or sleep just to escape the pleasant discipline of the U.S. Navy."[34]

"I am not going to send a single student of mine into the Navy until the Navy becomes a democratic institution," wrote a high school principal to Daniels. He added, "When will the officers of the Navy abandon the poppycock assumption of social superiority? I will not tolerate the old feudal constitution of the Navy in which officers are lords and the sailors villains."[35] Forced to confront this evidence that his view of life in the Navy as entirely educational and wholesome was rather far from reality, Daniels's usual practice was to label the complaints an exceptional case and point to the Navy's reenlistment rate as evidence that most sailors were fairly treated and happy.

Daniels's approach to the endemic problem of venereal disease in the Navy has been the subject of much comment. He banned the distribution of contraceptives and urged sailors to "keep themselves and their ships free from loathsome diseases." Prophylactics would act as "propaganda which tends to condone the sin of illicit sexual intercourse and engender in the young men of the Navy the belief that they have been provided with a method or means which will diminish the danger of unlawful or sinful misconduct."[36]

After the United States entered the war and thousands of new recruits entered the Navy, Daniels's anxieties increased. "Of all the sacrifices that have been made or that will be made for our country in this war, there is no sacrifice so heroic, so unselfish, so terrible as the sacrifice of the mother who sends her son in his strong, clean, young manhood from the protecting influence of his home to live, to fight and to die with no one near to guide or to advise him," Daniels declared in a wartime address. "Of all the responsibilities that are laid upon the civilian heads of the Army and Navy there is, after all, no responsibility more weighty, more solemn, more fraught with terrible results if evaded, than this responsibility of acting in a mother's place towards these splendid youths on whom the nation rests its hope of existence."[37]

With his well-developed sense of public relations, Daniels was soon leading a publicity and propaganda campaign against "moral misconduct." Under his direction the Navy prepared a pamphlet entitled "The Navy Will Fight to Protect True Womanhood," and another the following year called "Fit To Fight."[38] In addition the Navy Department produced a feature-length adventure film, *Cleared for Action,* designed to impress sailors with the dangers of sexual promiscuity.

The hero of *Cleared for Action* is Machinist Mate Ray Eldon, an aviator "with nothing to recommend him but a good, clear brain and clean, healthy body, untouched by any dissipation."[39] His pilot, Lieutenant Mel Carter, comes from a wealthy family but has serious character flaws. "His other self continually dragged him down to things earthy." While spending a final evening ashore, Ray manfully resists the invitations of his shipmates to get drunk and visit a bawdyhouse with them. Mel "succumbs to temptation, returns the worse for liquor and tumbles into his bunk without complying with the rules for prevention."

During the war Mel and Ray help to sink "a sneaking submarine" and become heroes. However, Mel discovers he has a venereal disease and is unable to save his fiancée with a blood donation. He attempts suicide. Ray becomes an officer and marries Mel's sister, Winnie, whom he had previously rescued from a boating accident. According to the script directions:

> The story fades from here and opens for the lesson:
> "WHICH LIFE WILL YOU FOLLOW?"
> Mel staring into space
> OR
> Ray and Winnie looking happily at each other and holding their young children.

While Daniels was battling the threat of venereal disease, Roosevelt became embroiled in a more doubtful crusade to "clean up" the Navy base at Newport, Rhode Island. Responding to reports that homosexuals, including a military chaplain, were attempting to pick up sailors at the naval training station, Roosevelt authorized and assisted a bizarre scheme to use sailors as undercover operatives to entrap suspects. Since the sailors were expected to engage in sex with the suspects in order to obtain evidence, it is debatable whether Daniels and Roosevelt could be said to be preventing or encouraging what they called "conditions of vice and depravity."

In the end, there was a scandal. Newport clergymen indignantly wrote to President Wilson that "a score of youths, enlisted in and wearing the uniform of the United States Navy, have been instructed in the details of a nameless vice and sent through the community to practice the same in general and in particular to entrap certain individuals."[40] A Senate investigation found the operation and Roosevelt's conduct "immoral and an abuse of his high office."

Sordid and irresponsible as it appeared, the Newport entrapment operations can be seen as the logical culmination of Daniels's and Roosevelt's insistence that they were acting not only as the highest civilian authority in the chain of command but *in loco parentis* and were therefore responsible for the character and morals of American sailors. Indeed, Roosevelt always spoke of the Newport entrapment operations as if they were simply a component of the department's commitment to clean up gambling, drugs, and prostitution.

Seen in perspective, the Daniels-Roosevelt era must be viewed not as a period of well-intentioned but naive and futile experiment but as the beginning of a modern approach to enlisted personnel policy that had close parallels in other navies. Daniels and Roosevelt, combining the democratizing, rationalizing, and technocratic aspects of the Progressive Era, laid the foundation for the competence-based, technology-oriented, specialized, and meritocratic navy of the twentieth century. Less happily, they also laid the foundation for the pervasive Big Brotherism of the modern military exemplified by compulsory ethics courses, surprise drug testing, and "don't ask, don't tell."

NOTES

1. Mildred Dewey to George Dewey, letter, n.d. 1913, George Goodwin Dewey Papers, Naval Historical Center.
2. Josephus Daniels, *The Wilson Era: Years of Peace, 1910-1917* (Chapel Hill: Univ. of North Carolina Press, 1944); Josephus Daniels, *The Wilson Era: Years of War and After, 1917-1923* (Chapel Hill: Univ. of North Carolina Press, 1946).
3. Ernest K. Lindley, *Franklin D. Roosevelt* (Indianapolis: Blue Ribbon Books, 1931), 56.
4. Carroll Kilpatrick, *Roosevelt and Daniels: A Friendship in Politics* (Chapel Hill: Univ. of North Carolina Press, 1952), 10.
5. Bradley A. Fiske, *From Midshipman to Rear Admiral* (New York: Century, 1919), 119.
6. Daniels, *Years of Peace*, 259.

7. Ted Morgan, *FDR: A Biography* (New York: Simon and Schuster, 1985), 152 and passim.

8. For Fisher's and Churchill's reforms, see Arthur J. Marder, *From the Dreadnought to Scapa Flow*, vol. 1; *The Road to War, 1904-1914* (London: Oxford Univ. Press, 1961) and Anthony Carew, *The Lower Deck of the Royal Navy* (Manchester: Manchester Univ. Press, 1981).

9. Herbert Gutman, *Work, Culture, and Society in Industrializing America* (New York: Knopf, 1976).

10. Filson Young, *With the Battle Cruisers* (London: Cassell, 1921), 65.

11. Norman E. Saul, *Sailors in Revolt: The Russian Baltic Fleet in 1917* (Lawrence, Kan.: Regents Press, 1976), 16.

12. Frederick S. Harrod, *Manning the New Navy* (Westport, Conn.: Greenwood Press, 1978), 29.

13. *Report of the Honorable Josephus Daniels, Secretary of the Navy*, 64th Cong., 1st Sess., March 30, 1916, 3554-65.

14. Daniels, *Years of Peace*, 255-56.

15. Commander William F. Fullam, "The System of Naval Training and Discipline Required to Promote Efficiency and Attract Americans," *U.S. Naval Institute Proceedings* 16 (1890): 479.

16. Harrod, *Manning the New Navy*, 18.

17. Unsigned memo to the Secretary of the Navy, Oct. 30, 1919, enclosing draft response to Honorable Rubin L. Haskell, M. C., Records of the Bureau of Naval Personnel, Morale Division, record group (RG) 24, National Archives.

18. Harrod, *Manning the New Navy*, 183-84.

19. Ibid., 59.

20. Daniels's handwritten draft of 1914 edition of *The Making of a Man-of-Wars Man*, Daniels Papers, Library of Congress, Washington, D.C.

21. *Report of the Secretary of the Navy*, 3554-65.

22. "U.S. Navy Rejects Man Sentenced to It to Reform Him," *New York American*, Aug. 25, 1915; Harrod, *Manning the New Navy*, 51, 55-56.

23. Harrod, *Manning the New Navy*, 68.

24. Ibid., 176-77.

25. Lieutenant Ridley R. McLean, "Permanency of the Enlisted Force of the Navy," *U.S. Naval Institute Proceedings* 32 (1906): 1261.

26. Harrod, *Manning the New Navy*, 180-81.

27. Daniels, "The Worth of Christian Character," Jan. 11, 1914, speech file, Daniels Papers.

28. George P. Dyer, "The Modern General Mess," *U.S. Naval Institute Proceedings* 32 (1906): 636.

29. Marder, *The Road to War*, 30-31.

30. Carew, *The Lower Deck*, 47-53; Captain John Wells, *The Royal Navy: An Illustrated Social History, 1870-1982* (Portsmouth: 1994), 87.

31. Daniels, *Years of Peace*, 274-75.

32. Harrod, *Manning the New Navy*, 106.

33. Anonymous letter from "Sailor USN" to editor, *Portsmouth Times-Record,* enclosure to J. F. Henry to Josephus Daniels, Jan. 3, 1914, Daniels Papers.
34. Felix Shay, "Felicitations," *The Era,* Apr. 1914, 4.
35. J. Remsan Bishop to Josephus Daniels, Nov. 19, 1913, Daniels Papers.
36. Daniels to Dr. George C. Stout, Dec. 17, 1917, file 26181.
37. RG 80, National Archives.
38. Daniels, "Men Must Live Straight to Shoot Straight," n.d. 1917, speech file, box 726, Daniels Papers.
39. Commander W. B. Anderson to Chief Pharmacist Mate J. Levansaler, Jul. 17, 1920, entry 415, RG 24, National Archives.
40. Script of *Cleared for Action,* by Bert Tracy, entry 410, box 35, RG 24, National Archives.
41. Morgan, *FDR,* 243.

FOUR

"Making It Easy For Him": The Imperial Japanese Navy and Franklin D. Roosevelt to Pearl Harbor

Michael A. Barnhart

IT IS HARD TO AVOID THE CONCLUSION that the Imperial Japanese Navy was one of Franklin Roosevelt's best friends right up to the "date which will live in infamy." After all, the Imperial Navy's surprise attack on Pearl Harbor gave Roosevelt the best justification conceivable for seeking and swiftly getting a nearly unanimous declaration of war from Congress and a furious and enthusiastic response from the American public. Despite some efforts by revisionist historians arguing that the Second World War revealed anew strains in the American social fabric, the facts are quite plain that there was no antiwar movement worthy of the name that Roosevelt ever had to contend with. So solid was American public opinion that Roosevelt was able to offer the significant token of unconditional (and no separate) surrender to America's allies in the war with no fear of a domestic backlash.

Perhaps as importantly, that Japan attacked any American territory at all on December 8 (Japan time) rescued Roosevelt from a promise that might have lived in infamy had the Japanese not been so accommodating. Less than a week earlier, Roosevelt had assured the British ambassador, Lord Halifax, that the United States approved a preemptive British occupation of Thai territory and would provide armed support in the event of a Japanese attack on British or Dutch possessions in the southwestern Pacific.[1] Even Roosevelt's most sympathetic biographers concede that this guarantee was extraconstitutional, and it seems at least likely that if the Japanese had confined their December offensive to British and Dutch territories, and if Roosevelt had committed American forces to the active defense of those territories, there would have been something of a discussion in Congress and among the public at large that might well have endorsed the president's actions in the end, but at a price of domestic discord and discontent that might have been steep.

Even earlier than December 1941, though, the Imperial Navy was Roosevelt's good friend. Perhaps Roosevelt could have gotten a declaration of war at the end of 1941 even if the Japanese had attacked solely Dutch and British possessions, but it seems virtually impossible that he could have committed the United States to such a guarantee over a year earlier—in the spring of 1940, when in fact Japan first seriously debated whether to attack them. A Japanese blitz in the southwestern Pacific, following hard upon Germany's stunning successes in Scandinavia, the Low Countries, and France, might not have led to an inevitable victory for the antidemocratic powers, but it would have made the defeat of at least Great Britain much more conceivable, not to mention the collapse of Nationalist China.

Last and, to be honest, probably least, Franklin Roosevelt would have had a harder task in persuading Congress to fund the resurgence of the United States Navy in the late 1930s without the seemingly willful disregard toward the cause of peace or arms limitations displayed by an increasingly truculent Imperial Navy. While it may go too far to argue that the Imperial Navy was primarily responsible for the construction of the ships that it would encounter in the opening rounds of the Pacific war, from the Java Sea to Midway, it seems fair to maintain that Japan's clumsy hostility toward the West and quite blatant cruelty toward China made Roosevelt's task of getting those ships built easier than it otherwise would have been.

What makes these stances all the more difficult to understand is the simple fact that the senior officers of the Imperial Navy ought to have known better, much better. These officers took deliberate pride in their knowledge of the United States, and especially the United States Navy. The path to flag rank for Imperial Navy officers almost invariably included a tour of duty in America, and often several.[2] Yamamoto Isoroku, for example, was stationed in the United States from 1919 to 1921 while he was a commander and, from 1926 to 1928, Yamamoto served as naval attaché in Washington at captain's rank.[3] Japan's Naval Staff College rivaled Newport and Annapolis in its discussions, debates, and even applications of the theories of American naval strategist Alfred Thayer Mahan.[4]

Yet, by the time Franklin Roosevelt became president in 1933, the Imperial Navy contributed much more to increased friction with the United States than to any attempts at understanding. In fact, the Imperial Navy never attempted an understanding of Roosevelt's increasingly delicate political and diplomatic position throughout the 1930s, or even in the critical years of 1940 and 1941, in order to complicate Roosevelt's position to Japan's advantage. Instead, its policies dramatically eased the president's position. The Imperial Navy always "made it easy" for him. Why?

Two hypotheses can be ruled out quickly. The officers of the Imperial Navy were not ignorant, nor were they stupid. Admissions standards at Etajima (Japan's Annapolis) were astonishingly strict, and only those graduating near the top of their class could hope to attend the Naval Staff College. Its graduates, lest we need any reminding, led a service that operated the Zero fighter, the Long Lance torpedo, and the battleship *Yamato*. It was a service that had trained the best carrier pilots and night surface-fleet fighters in the world by the start of the Pacific war.

Nor can we attribute the Imperial Navy's mulishness to American hostility toward Japan throughout Roosevelt's presidency. To be sure, relations between Tokyo and Washington were strained upon Roosevelt's coming to office, the result of the Imperial Army's desire to protect its position in Manchuria in 1931 and the Imperial Navy's self-proclaimed protection of Japanese interests in Shanghai a year later. But from 1933 to at least the start of 1940—a pretty long run— it seems fair to say that the Roosevelt administration did not act in an overly provocative way. As many historians (some of them represented in this volume) have noted, the American reaction to Japan's consolidation of Manchuria, and further encroachment into north China proper, was quite muted.[5] The American reaction to Japan's abrogation of the naval arms limitation treaties signed at Washington and London was more a shrug than a protest.[6] Japan's undeclared war against China, starting in July 1937, drew American protests but no more, even after Japanese forces massacred Chinese civilians at Nanking by that year's end and sank an American gunboat during the proceedings. Nor was American naval construction exactly booming during these years.

If not Japanese stupidity or American provocation, then what does account for the apparent blindness of the Imperial Navy during Roosevelt's presidency? The central cause of the Imperial Navy's improbable policies leading up to the Second World War was the impossible institutional dilemma that confronted its leadership during the First World War. That dilemma was this: The First World War had shown that the very best fighting machines in the world were useless without the resources and industry to build and operate them. The best technical plans for planes, ships, guns, and torpedoes meant nothing if these could not be built, and built in very substantial numbers. Even once built, the very best battleship or carrier or destroyer was useless without fuel (and that increasingly meant fuel oil) to run it. Yet Japan had virtually no iron ore or oil, and the nearest sources seemed easily disrupted by the Imperial Navy's likeliest future enemies, the British and the Americans.

Japan essentially had two choices. It could embark upon a bold, costly, and surely risky program of territorial expansion abroad and industrial expansion at home to acquire the ways and means to support a large fleet in the age of total war. Or it could reconcile itself to an Asian and Pacific role frankly subordinate to the Western maritime powers.

Neither choice was very palatable for the Imperial Navy. A campaign of aggressive territorial and industrial expansion raised the possibility of a war against the West that Japan could not expect to win until it had completed that campaign of expansion—a dilemma of its own that admitted no easy solution. As badly, the Imperial Navy simply lacked the political influence and organizational ability to embark upon such a campaign even if it wished to. Such a program instead would have to be undertaken by the Imperial Navy's most loathed rival, the Imperial Japanese Army. Would the army, once it had acquired territory—under its control—and built up industry—under its control—share its resources and factories with the navy? Many senior admirals of the early 1920s were doubtful and, for these reasons, strongly supported the treaties limiting warship construction signed at Washington in 1922 and London in 1930. Why, they asked, engage in a construction race Japan could not win? Why not limit Western, especially American, naval strength as a way to limit Western and American influence over core Japanese interests in East Asia?[7]

Because, younger naval officers argued, these naval treaties relegated Japan to a subordinate status, under America and Britain, and because they made painfully clear the ugly truth that the Imperial Navy was not and—so long as the treaties were in force— never could be a "real" navy that might be expected to fight precisely those nations that had the most to gain by challenging Japan's position and interests in East Asia. A "treaty navy" was a sham force that existed only at the sufferance of the West.[8]

These younger officers of the 1920s were not so young by the 1930s. After a bitter controversy that saw Japan ratify the London Treaty in 1930, they moved successfully to overthrow the older leaders who had favored accommodation with the West. But they could not overthrow the central truths that resided at the core of the Imperial Navy's fundamental plight. Very well, there would not be any accommodation with the West. There would be renewed warship construction and, of course, the possibility of war for a "real" navy. But how was Japan to ever keep pace if the Americans decided to sprint? And how could the Imperial Navy realistically hope to defeat the Americans if war ever did come?

As a result of the Roosevelt administration's largely passive policy toward Japan, these irksome questions were not faced for the balance of the thirties. Staff studies and wargames showed that the Imperial Navy could weaken the American fleet by aggressive attrition caused by submarines and land-based air as that fleet worked its way toward the western Pacific. Once there, the Japanese warrior spirit would prevail over the materialistic Yankees already demoralized by their prior losses.[9]

But by the spring of 1940 this pat scenario had been shattered by swift-moving events in Europe and reactions to them in America. Neither the first Vinson plan of 1934 for American warship construction nor the second of 1938 had caused much concern in Imperial Navy circles. But the third Vinson plan, which Congress authorized in June 1940, was another matter entirely. Any Japanese response would require a construction program of unprecedented scope, a scope that worsened the Imperial Navy's strategic dilemma to intolerable levels.

All Japan barely had enough iron and steel (and foreign exchange to import more iron, usually as scrap) to even commence a building plan to counter the third Vinson plan. But the Imperial

Navy hardly had access to all Japanese resources or foreign exchange. The Imperial Army had been bogged down in a rapidly expanding conflict with China for nearly three years. It had fought major battles against the Soviet Union's Red Army in 1938 at Changkufeng and 1939 at Nomonhan, had been thrashed soundly both times, and was looking for revenge, hopefully with German help. All these efforts had consumed and were consuming immense quantities of iron, steel, and oil—all of which the Imperial Navy desperately needed. Yet it was not very likely that the army could be persuaded to forego defensive measures against the Soviets or withdraw from Chinese territory bought at such a costly price. How was the Imperial Navy to compel a redirection of Japan's increasingly scant resources to its rapidly mushrooming requirements?

The obvious answer was extortion and the obvious victim the Imperial Army. Fortunately for the Imperial Navy, the army badly wanted two things in the spring and summer of 1940 that required the navy's consent: the alliance with Germany and an attack southward (the so-called Southward Advance) against the newly defenseless colonies of French Indochina, British Malaya, and the Dutch East Indies.[10]

The Imperial Army's desire for an alliance with Germany was hardly new in mid-1940, but it was more urgent than ever. It was certain to bolster Japan's position against the Soviet Union. It also would further demoralize China, which could hope less and less for either Western or Soviet aid, and at last might allow the army to extricate itself from that quagmire. Better yet, it would ease the way for a Japanese occupation of those European colonies rich in oil and other resources.

The Imperial Navy was willing to agree to the alliance, if it received sharply increased allocations of oil and steel from Japan's immediate reserves. As for a Southward Advance in the summer or fall of 1940, the navy steadfastly refused. This was a refusal that stemmed directly from the Imperial Navy's central dilemma. Although it was quite prepared to use its consent to the Southward

Advance to extort still more oil and steel from the army, it was not prepared to risk war with the United States even after receiving more of these resources. The Imperial Army rather logically proposed a Southward Advance that did not include any American targets, only the European colonies. The Imperial Navy strongly objected, arguing that America would never desert Britain, and that an American fleet presence in the Philippines would render any territorial gains in Malaya or the East Indies impossible to enjoy. Put another way, for the navy the only conceivable Southward Advance was one that included war against America.

How did the Imperial Navy arrive at this assessment? Was it through a judicious tracking of Anglo-American relations through the critical summer of 1940? Did the Imperial Navy coolly calculate that the emerging relationship between sea dogs Churchill and Roosevelt precluded any possibility of attempting an attack upon solely European territory? While additional research is always possible and desirable, it seems clear that the Imperial Navy did not closely follow the Battle of Britain and American debates over whether to aid London or let it go. Instead, the Imperial Navy had no choice but to assert, as it put it, "Anglo-American indivisibility." Here is the reason: If the Southward Advance could be executed against only French, British, and Dutch holdings, why would the Imperial Navy have any need for more oil or steel? Why would it have to engage in a naval race with the Americans? If, as the Imperial Army had argued, the German alliance really worked, and America was either paralyzed and kept to itself in the Western Hemisphere or, at worst, threw what military it had into the Atlantic, what need was there for much of an Imperial Navy at all?

So the Southward Advance had to include war against the United States. This stance gained warship materials for the navy, but left its dilemma more painfully apparent than ever. By the start of 1941, increasing numbers of rear admirals and captains were demanding a resolution to the dilemma by asserting that the navy should resolutely determine to make war upon the Americans and beat them. The time was right. The United States would have no allies worth the name. Its colossal third Vinson program was far from completed. It was distracted by German successes in Europe.[11]

In fact, by the spring of 1941 those German successes gave fresh urgency to the Imperial Navy to actively advocate a South-ward Advance—including war with the United States—that it had resisted just a year before. Reports of an impending German attack on the Soviet Union had led the Imperial Army to try to cancel the Southward Advance in favor of crash preparations in Manchuria for a northward attack into the Maritime Provinces and Siberia to eliminate the Soviet menace once and for all. However attractive this option was to the army, to the Imperial Navy it was anathema since it would have spelled an immediate and radical readjustment of resource and materials allocations strongly back to the army's favor. Over the longer term, it would have meant at best a long delay in the implementation of the Southward Advance, allowing the Americans to complete their third Vinson plan while the Imperial Navy, in contrast, suspended new construction.[12]

It should not be surprising that Naval Chief of Staff Admiral Nagano Osami bluntly advocated war against Britain and the United States in mid-June, just before the onset of the German attack and well before the Americans imposed any embargo on oil that, according to some accounts, drove Japan into a desperate attack on the West. Nor should it be surprising that the Imperial Army strongly opposed any such Southward Advance. The result-ing compromise was an interservice agreement to keep all options open for the time being. The army would rush reinforcements to Manchuria to take advantage of any sudden Soviet collapse, but the Southward Advance would be kept alive through the occupation of bases in southern French Indochina.

As is well known, Franklin Roosevelt became aware of the decision to seek these bases through the Magic code-breaking operation. Magic did not pick up news of the reinforcement of

Manchuria, but Roosevelt correctly deduced that the Japanese, as he put it, were having a "dragdown and knockout" over which way to jump. His response was a freeze of Japanese assets in the United States to restrain Japanese moves both north and south.[13] For a number of reasons, this freeze rapidly escalated into a full-scale trade embargo, shutting off oil to Japan, and at least bringing the Imperial Navy's dilemma to a head.

At least in this respect, though, Roosevelt's altered policy was a friend of the Imperial Navy's. Even the most die-hard generals of the Imperial Army had to concede that a northward advance was impossible until Japan had secured its own supplies of oil. A final army-navy dispute was resolved firmly in the Imperial Navy's favor: the Southward Advance would include an attack—indeed an opening attack—upon the Philippines(and, unknown to the army, Hawaii as well) to ensure that America was in the fight and, of course, the Imperial Navy had a role, with the resource and materials allocations increased appropriately. From August through November 1941 the navy's leadership still wriggled on the horns of its dilemma, hoping that the Americans would capitulate to Japan's basic terms in the so-called Hull-Nomura negotiations, hoping that the Imperial Navy in fact would not have to fight.[14] That autumn the navy leadership repeatedly stalled a final decision to attack, to the army's immense frustration. But in the end the admirals could hardly admit that their extortion had been to no purpose. It was time to capitulate themselves or fight and take their chances. They chose to roll the dice.

Franklin Roosevelt, indeed any American policymaker or policy, is strikingly absent from this talk. Does this mean that, with the exception of the nature and timing of the oil embargo, the administration could have had little real influence over the course of the Imperial Navy and Japan in general? The answer must be "yes." The United States might have capitulated and betrayed at the least China and the Dutch East Indies. Such a surrender would have rescued the Imperial Navy from its dilemma rather nicely. Or

Roosevelt might have weakened the United States Navy so much before 1941 that Japan might have compelled a similar American capitulation by force of arms sometime in 1942. But these scenarios seem very far-fetched.

Could Roosevelt have resolved the dilemma by demonstrating to the Imperial Navy that going to war against America was completely hopeless, that the dice would always come up snake eyes? This too seems very doubtful. The Imperial Navy received consistently excellent reports from its attachés in Washington, the most recent (Captain Yokoyama Ichiro) a good personal friend of Rear Admiral Richmond Kelly Turner.[15] These men consistently warned against any prospects of hope in a war against America. In the end, though, they could do nothing to overthrow the stark truth that to admit to such an outcome left the Imperial Navy no place in the empire. And so came the crap shoot and the shooting on that fateful Sunday morning.

NOTES

1. Recent coverage of this assurance appears in Waldo Heinrichs, *Threshold of War: Franklin D. Roosevelt and American Entry into World War Two* (New York: Oxford Univ. Press, 1988), 216-17. One of the earliest accounts to suggest that Roosevelt had made such a promise is Raymond A. Esthus, "President Roosevelt's Commitment to Britain to Intervene in a Pacific War," *Mississippi Valley Historical Review* 50 (1963): 28-38.
2. These career paths may be traced in Nihon Kindai Shiryo Kenkyukai, ed., *Nihon Roku-Kaigun no seido, soshiki, jinji* (Tokyo: Tokyo Daiguku Shippankai, 1971).
3. Hiroyuki Agawa, *The Reluctant Admiral: Yamamoto and the Imperial Navy* (Tokyo: Kodansha International, Ltd., 1979), i.
4. Asada Sadao, *Ryotaisen kan no Nichi-Bei kankei: Kaigun to seisaku kettei* (Tokyo: Tokyo Daigaku Shuppankai, 1993), chap. 1.
5. The standard account for these years is Dorothy Borg, *The United States and the Far Eastern Crisis of 1933-1938* (Cambridge: Harvard Univ. Press, 1964).
6. Stephen E. Pelz, *Race to Pearl Harbor: The Failure of the Second London Naval Conference and the Onset of World War II* (Cambridge: Harvard Univ. Press, 1974), chap. 11.

7. Asada Sadao, "From Washington to London: The Imperial Japanese Navy and the Politics of Naval Limitation, 1921-1930," *Diplomacy and Statecraft* 43 (1993): 147-91.

8. Asada Sadao, "The Japanese Navy and the United States," in *Pearl Harbor as History: Japanese-American Relations, 1931 1941*, ed , Dorothy Borg and Shumpei Okamoto (New York: Columbia Univ. Press, 1973).

9. Pelz, *Race to Pearl Harbor,* 34-40.

10. Michael A. Barnhart, *Japan Prepares for Total War: The Search for Economic Security, 1919-1941* (Ithaca: Cornell Univ. Press, 1987), chap. 9.

11. Asada, "Imperial Navy," 248-52.

12. Asada, "Imperial Navy," 252-56; Barnhart, *Japan Prepares,* chap. 11.

13. Heinrichs, *Threshold of War,* 124-34; Jonathan G. Utley, *Going to War with Japan, 1937-1941* (Knoxville: Univ. of Tennessee Press, 1985), 151-56. For "dragdown and knockout," see William L. Langer and S. Everett Gleason, *The Undeclared War, 1940-1941* (New York: Harper & Brothers, 1953), 647.

14. Admiral Nomura Kichisaburo had been designated as Japan's ambassador to the United States in November 1940 in hopes that his personal friendship with Franklin Roosevelt would defuse Japanese-American tensions and permit, among other things, Japan's successful resolution of the fighting with China. Concerned that Nomura and the Imperial Japanese Navy would grant unacceptable concessions to the Americans over China, the Imperial Army dispatched Colonel Iwakuro Hideo as a watchdog in the spring of 1941. For a detailed treatment of the Hull-Nomura talks, see Robert J. C. Butow, *The John Doe Associates: Backdoor Diplomacy for Peace, 1941* (Stanford: Stanford Univ. Press, 1974). Unfortunately, Nomura's postwar memoirs of these negotiations are unhelpful concerning both his personal relationship with Roosevelt and his feelings toward the army and Iwakuro. Nomura Kichisaburo, *Beikoku ni tsukaishite: Nihon gaiko no kaiko* (Tokyo: Iwanamiu shoten, 1946).

15. Asada, "Imperial Navy," 257.

FIVE

FRANKLIN ROOSEVELT AND NAVAL STRATEGY, 1933-1941

Jonathan G. Utley

A PRESIDENT CAN PLAY SEVERAL DIFFERENT ROLES in respect to national security. He can be an inspiring force setting the tone, he can be a hands-on planner, he can even be the ringmaster of a three-ring circus as Tom Hone suggests FDR was. But whatever style of leadership he might have, I suggest that a president also must have certain minimal managerial skills. I suggest three criteria by which we might judge any president's managerial skills.

First, the president must make sure that the ends of national policy and the means available to achieve those ends are in balance or he must work to bring them into balance. An administration that establishes national strategic objectives that exceed the national power is asking for trouble.

Second, if the president is contemplating a strategic plan different from that approved by his national security structure, he needs to share his thoughts with the national security planners so that the president's ideas can be integrated into the strategic plan. At a moment of crisis, the president who recommends a strategic plan he likes but no one else has planned for is only creating confusion and the likelihood of hasty and unplanned actions.

Third, as the chief executive, the president is obligated to see that the different parts of the national security structure agree on the strategic plan. In the pre–World War II days, the national strategic structure was, for the most part, limited to the State, War, and Navy Departments. While there can be the greatest amount of latitude given to different elements within this structure when it debates policy, at some point a decision has to be reached and the various parts have to work together to achieve national policy.

Examining Franklin Roosevelt during the increasingly troubled years of 1933-1941, I think the preponderance of evidence indicates that he was not a satisfactory manager of strategic policy. He failed to meet the test in each of the three areas outlined above. He came closest in balancing ends and means. But he had a bad habit of springing on the Navy Department plans that no one had considered. And he was notorious for allowing different departments to work at cross-purposes.

The debate over just how good a policy manager Franklin Roosevelt was has lasted longer than his presidency. Critics have complained that the New Deal was not a plan for recovery but a mishmash of programs in which different people with different ideas of how to progress were given presidential approval to proceed even though they might be working at cross-purposes or, at the very least, basing their programs on mutually exclusive theories of recovery.

That diversity of approach can also be seen in the interface between domestic and foreign policies. After gathering a cabinet of brain trusters devoted to economic nationalism, Roosevelt selected a secretary of state who demanded of the president, and was promised, a free hand to move the nation toward economic internationalism.

Was this FDR's genius, to devise a plan that would try a variety of approaches in the hope that one of them would prove effective in ameliorating the crisis confronting the nation? Or was the opposite extreme true, that the president had no stomach for making his government work in harmony? Roosevelt certainly said that he had a plan and that he knew what was happening. In his fireside chat in May 1933, the president asserted, "The legislation which has been passed or is in the process of enactment can properly be considered as part of a well-grounded plan." And in a closed meeting of the National Emergency Council in December 1934 he took some pains to let everyone know that the great web of domestic programs he was weaving could be understood only by one man, Franklin D. Roosevelt: "We have a great many people working," he explained, "and no one person knows what the other person is doing, except myself—right here, nowhere else in the government."[1]

The master strategist was at work! Or so the president would have us believe.

Admittedly, Franklin Roosevelt was in uncharted waters when it came to rescuing the nation from the Great Depression. But in the area of strategic planning, the president had considerable experience. To begin with, FDR was a Navy man who loved and understood the Navy; it was his hobby. Moreover, he had a worldview based on a belief that American prosperity and security depended upon access to the raw materials and markets of the world. This was a view that corresponded to the view of many naval officers. Ultimately, both Roosevelt and the Navy understood, it was up to the United States Navy to protect these vital American interests, and they agreed that the challenge would come from Japan. It was only a matter of time before Japan moved to close Western access to the vast markets and raw materials of Asia, and when it did, the United States Navy would have to intervene.

To meet this challenge, Navy strategists drafted a war plan code named Orange for Japan. War Plan Orange was in place before Roosevelt came into office, so the president did not have to approve it. But as a strategy, it was something less than realistic. Though the ebb and flow of bureaucratic eddies within the Navy led to modifications and reconsideration of options in Plan Orange, the basic idea was to confront Japan in the western Pacific. But that required ships and advanced, fortified naval and air bases that the United States did not have. Indeed, Admiral James O. Richardson characterized War Plan Orange as less a plan for waging war than a plan to justify building a navy.

As Thomas Hone shows in his contribution to this volume, Roosevelt did support naval construction and the development of technology related to naval forces. But this support was not so great as to bring naval power into line with naval objectives. Nor was the president more successful in providing for the naval and air bases that the planned offensive move across the Pacific Ocean would require. In 1935, when discussions on independence for the Philippines were underway, naval officers in Washington asked the president to set aside naval bases in the Philippines that the United States would retain after Philippine independence. Roosevelt refused to do so. From the Navy's perspective the United States either had to have naval bases from which it could operate or it had to surrender any hope of controlling the western Pacific. But FDR was more ambivalent. He responded that it was not then necessary to make a decision and that he had doubts such bases could be defended. Waldo Heinrichs has characterized the president's response to the Navy as one of doubt and indecision.[2] The president showed no greater leadership when it came to developing either naval or naval air bases in islands such as Guam or Wake.[3]

In 1935, Roosevelt could afford to be indecisive on this topic. There was no pressing military confrontation, and even if the president had sought funds for establishing naval bases in the Philippines, Guam, or even Wake Island, it was doubtful that Congress would have provided them. And there can be no doubt that during the first Roosevelt administration, there were far more pressing issues than ones of naval strategy. We must always keep in mind that a president, even one as energetic as Franklin Roosevelt, is a single person with limited time. Not every issue could receive his full attention. But as the situation in the world deteriorated in the later 1930s, the case for benign neglect cannot so easily be made. Even then, presidential leadership in enhancing military capability remained limited. Nor did FDR show any interest in tampering with war plans prior to the outbreak of war in Europe.[4]

It is possible that this was Roosevelt the sly fox, fully aware that the nation did not possess the resources to successfully carry out Plan Orange but also knowing that the mere existence of the plan made obtaining naval appropriations from Congress much easier. Or it is possible that the President, aware that the United States did not and would not have the power to stop Japan, believed that a continued national presence in East Asia, albeit less than what was desirable, would have a restraining influence on Japan, while a withdrawal from that region would encourage Japanese expansion far sooner than would otherwise be the case. Add to this an astute reading of the isolationist feeling in the land and we can make a case for FDR the pragmatic leader who was getting as much as he could.

But the same evidence could lead one to conclude that Franklin Roosevelt always liked to keep his options open, which is a nice way of saying he would put off making a decision until he had to. This caution had served him very well in the political arena. But in the area of strategic planning, with its long lead time for implementation, postponing decisions until crises developed was fraught with danger.

It is important to draw the distinction between thinking strategically, which Roosevelt was quite capable of doing, and seeing that a strategic plan was drafted, which was the kind of thing FDR shunned. In fact, grand strategy in its most global form was something the president enjoyed. What he disdained was leading the Navy or Army to revise a particular war plan. There are exceptions to this generalization. The most notable one was in 1940 and 1941 when the president devised and micromanaged the implementation of a naval policy in the Atlantic. But for the most part, detailing strategic plans was too bothersome to receive his attention. When he thought strategically, he painted a broad canvas with little thought given to the details. The result was a series of unfinished paintings.

One incident that clearly reveals this aspect of the president's approach to strategic planning was the so-called Quarantine Speech of October 1937. The speech, delivered in the heartland of isolationism, was a calculated move to wean the nation away from the storm-cellar isolationism that tied the administration's hands in the area of foreign policy. In that sense, the speech was standard internationalist fare, arguing that the United States could not ignore what was happening elsewhere in the world. The sting in the tail was a reference to quarantining aggressor states, and that was put there by the president himself. It reflected the president's frustration with a naval strategy that presumed a full-scale war with Japan that was provoked by Japan on the one hand and distressingly futile diplomatic protests on the other. He was not prepared to go to war over Japanese outrages in China nor was he prepared to sit quietly by and do nothing. He sought a strategy that was as forceful as that of the aggressors, and as cunning as was their policy of always taking actions short of war.[5]

But I think in talking quarantine, FDR was giving vent to his strategy of choice. It was an approach he had voiced before and would return to again. And it was nothing like the strategy enshrined in War Plan Orange. Had Roosevelt developed a strategy in any detail, it would have involved a combination of commercial sanctions cutting off trade between Japan and the United States and naval blockade to end trade with the rest of the world. In Roosevelt's mind, this was the creative employment of power, effective yet short of war.

The president had recommended this strategy to the British when German armies occupied the demilitarized Rhineland; German troops occupying German soil. Paralyzed by fear of a war, the European powers arrayed against Germany did not immediately respond. FDR suggested in an informal conversation that the British should shut down all commerce into and out of Germany, using the continental powers to close the German border on the continent and the British navy to seal it off by sea. Faced with this combined front, he thought, Germany would back down.[6] That Britain was unwilling to take this risk did not diminish FDR's faith in the strategy of encirclement. It was the backbone behind his quarantine speech.

To be sure, the president said nothing in his speech about deploying naval power. And he mentioned only tightening economic pressure on Japan through commercial sanctions when he briefed Ambassador-at-Large Norman H. Davis a few days later. Davis headed the U.S. delegation to the Brussels Conference, a conference of Nine-Power Treaty signatories called to deal with the problem of Japan in China. By the time that conference opened, the American public had grown nervous about the entangling nature of a quarantine and the president would not consider deployment of naval power. He did not even support Davis at Brussels and let the conference adjourn without taking any action against Japan.

But the idea of employing naval force to isolate Japan lingered in the president's mind. His thoughts of a string of ships from the Aleutian Islands to Singapore that would stop the flow of goods into and out of Japan was reinforced by a letter from Commander in Chief, Asiatic Fleet, Admiral Harry E. Yarnell. Then in December 1937, when the U.S. gunboat *Panay* was sunk on the Yangtze River by Japanese naval aircraft, FDR returned to the idea again.

As he contemplated how to respond to this most provocative Japanese act, the president suggested a string of warships from the Aleutian Islands to the Philippines cooperating with a string of British warships from the Philippines to Singapore. Sitting a thousand miles from the Japanese home islands, these ships would cut off the flow of goods into and out of Japan and bring that aggressor state to its knees in a year to 18 months. There seems to have been little if any consideration given to how Japan might respond to this act of war. The president even suggested this approach to the British ambassador and dispatched Captain Royal Ingersoll to London to enter into talks. But when Ingersoll arrived, the British realized that he was not charged with planning a blockade but only to begin discussing contingency plans for Anglo-American naval cooperation.[7]

By the start of 1938, the president had shown that he had doubts about the feasibility, and certainly the utility, of a naval strategy dependent on War Plan Orange and that he favored a policy of encirclement and strangulation. But that policy was not developed in 1938. The president did not instruct the Navy to devise a plan by which Japanese trade could be interdicted. He did not make Ingersoll's visit to London the opening phase of a concerted effort to establish an Anglo-American naval plan to deter Japanese expansion. To be sure, Anglo-American staff talks would eventually develop, but for some time there was a clear difference between existing naval strategy put forward in War Plan Orange and what the president preferred, and no one did anything to bridge that gap.

A string of ships across the Pacific was not the only naval strategy the president contemplated. In the summer of 1939, the U.S. ambassador to Japan, Joseph C. Grew, warned the president that increased economic pressure might lead Japan to strike south and seize the raw materials it required. The president blithely responded that in such a case, the U.S. Navy would intercept the Japanese navy.[8] This was classic FDR. He could brush aside a serious problem with an off-the-cuff comment. Perhaps he had no intention of intercepting the Japanese fleet and was simply offering a comment that would dismiss Grew's warnings. But with war clouds hanging very low indeed over Europe, it seemed probable that in the near future Britain would be preoccupied in Europe and the Asian balance of power upset. It would seem prudent, in that situation, to have some plans for responding to a Japanese move into the South Pacific. But we do not find the president going to his

War and Navy Departments protesting that he needed more flexibility than Plan Orange gave him.

Consequently, in the spring of 1940, as the world situation went from bad to worse, the president sought to act, but without a strategic plan available that suited the situation. The problem was the German spring offensive. Whatever else that offensive accomplished, Holland would fall before the German armies and thus the Dutch East Indies, rich with oil and coveted by Japan, would be vulnerable. As the Japanese began to show increased interest in those islands, Washington worried that Japan would move south to seize the Dutch oil. The Roosevelt administration was not prepared to stand by and allow that to happen. A new, tougher tone entered Secretary of State Hull's public and private statements to Japan. But to FDR's mind, tough words had to be backed up with naval pressure. The United States had to do something to prevent the Japanese expansion southward. Unfortunately, the president did not have an arsenal of naval strategies to draw upon.

Three types of strategies existed for Roosevelt to follow. One was full-scale warfare, and for that he had a plan, Plan Orange. Another was long-range blockade and economic strangulation. No planning had been done to implement that kind of confrontation. A third was a deterrent effected by placing the fleet in a position that was threatening enough to stop Japanese expansion. Did that mean moving it to Singapore or the Philippines or Australia or fortifying Guam as a more advanced base of operations? The careful planning that would have gone into any such strategy was never undertaken because FDR did not ask for such studies to be made.

Having no plan did not prevent the president from implementing naval action. Roosevelt decided to deploy the Pacific Fleet to Pearl Harbor, 2,000 miles closer to Japan.

As was its norm each spring, the fleet was in Hawaiian waters honing its combat skills, and FDR had only to instruct that it not return to its old home base in California. He made the switch with no fanfare, so that it would not appear to be too provocative to Japan (or to isolationist forces in the United States). But the decision to transfer the fleet was not a decision to put into effect some larger plan of operations. There was no plan, just an order. It was a move that the fleet commander in chief, Admiral J. O. Richardson, protested in the most strenuous terms.[9] Without the mobilization of the Navy there would not be the supply ships to enable the fleet to operate away from Pearl Harbor. Moreover, sitting at Pearl, the fleet was exposed and lacked adequate facilities for training.

The decision had all the earmarks of being, to use the language of the time, a horseback decision. It was not part of a larger plan or naval strategy, simply an isolated action taken with no prior consultation or careful review of the consequences.

The Netherlands fell to the German armies as expected, but so did just about everything else in Europe. The survival of Britain was now in question and thus the continued existence of the Royal Navy was in doubt. Roosevelt, whose interest in Europe had always outweighed his interest in Asia, increasingly turned his attention to Europe and the Atlantic. But the change in the Navy's focus was far more extreme. Though there had been no clear presidential directive to fashion alternative strategies for deterring Japanese expansion, Navy planners had been contemplating small-scale actions to give Japan pause. Captain R. S. Crenshaw, Director of Naval War Plans, was considering a courtesy visit of U.S. destroyers to the Netherlands East Indies. But when France collapsed, he turned his attention to contingency plans for the Atlantic should Britain go under. By June 1940, the Navy had all but abandoned the Pacific and was designing plans for transferring substantial parts of the Pacific Fleet to the Atlantic.[10]

This transformation kept the Navy in harmony with the president. It also brought the president into closer contact with the Navy over just how to operate in the Atlantic. Making up policy as he went, carefully weighing the diplomatic and domestic political situations, Roosevelt fashioned a course of naval action in the Atlantic that demonstrated that when he wanted to, he could play a very hands-on role in both strategic and tactical planning. Waldo Heinrichs and others have carefully examined this phase of Roosevelt's management of naval policy and have convincingly argued that naval action went forward when the president said it should and slowed down when the president wanted to wait. It was a deliberate policy, not one of drift.[11]

Whether or not we like the plan Roosevelt implemented for the Atlantic, he deserves high marks for fashioning a strategic plan and seeing it to fruition. But as far as strategic planning is concerned, FDR's Atlantic planning was the exception to the rule. Even while carefully evolving his Atlantic strategy, the president gave vent to his penchant for letting different parts of his administration head off in different directions. The issue was over what in the Pacific the United States would go to war for.

Chief of Naval Operations Harold R. Stark was very clear that the security of the United States rested in the Atlantic. Though he was confident that the president shared this view, there were many in Washington who would focus American efforts elsewhere, particularly against Japan. Stark decided to take the lead in drafting a war plan that would place first things first. He started on a Saturday in October 1940, worked through the night, and spent the next ten days polishing the new war plan with his staff. It is instructive that this was Stark's baby, created from his mind on his initiative. Clearly the president's interest in the Atlantic encouraged Stark to draft this new plan, but it was not taken at the instructions of the president. The leadership came from the CNO.

Stark based his strategy on the assumption that Europe was vital to American national security. He believed that only if the United States threw its support behind Britain could Germany be stopped and Europe saved. He reviewed the options available to the United States in various war plans that existed and were contemplated. A hemispheric defense scheme would not bring about Germany's defeat. A Plan Orange kind of offensive against Japan or even the old Rooseveltian concept of a long-range cruiser and submarine war of attrition would not work because either would divert precious resources away from the fundamental problem: defeat of Germany. In the event of war with Japan, he concluded, the only alternative was the fourth one, plan D or Plan Dog: Stand on the defensive in the Pacific while winning the war in the Atlantic.[12]

Having gained the Army's support for this strategy (the Army had never liked the idea of fighting in Asia or the Pacific), Stark went to the president for an endorsement, FDR style. No formal endorsement was sought; it was sufficient for FDR to nod his approval. The president gave his blessing and War Plan Rainbow 5 was developed, a plan that called for the United States to write off much of the South Pacific until the primary enemy, Germany, could be defeated. Buoyed by this presidential approval, U.S. naval officers entered into discussions with their British counterparts over naval efforts and held a firm line against diverting any attention away from the Atlantic theater. Southeast Asia and the South Pacific were vital to the British war effort, British admirals proclaimed; these areas simply were not expendable. American officers replied that they may be vital to the preservation of the British Empire but not to winning the war against Germany.[13]

The real problem came not because British and American naval officers disagreed but from the lack of coordination between the civilian elements of the Roosevelt administration who controlled foreign policy and the naval elements who would fight the war. The position of the Department of State was that Japanese expansion into the South Pacific and Southeast Asia was intolerable. Foreign-policy managers were not absolutely certain precisely where the line would be drawn but they were certain that there was a point where vital U.S. interests were involved and the United States would go to war. But the Navy and Plan Rainbow 5 wrote off the very interests that the State Department considered a *casus belli*. To put it in concrete terms, the diplomats contended that the United States would have to go to war with Japan to prevent that expansionist state from seizing the Netherlands East Indies, while Stark's plan was based on the assumption that the Indies were not worth fighting for.

Roosevelt did nothing to resolve this conflict. In fact, his actions simply exacerbated the situation. On January 16, 1941, the president gave his formal approval to the Plan Dog strategy. But only five days after embracing Plan Dog, Roosevelt signed a letter to Ambassador Grew praising the ambassador for his analysis of the importance of defending Singapore. In Anglo-American naval staff talks, the American naval officers had adamantly refused to accept the defense of Singapore as vital. Rainbow 5 was based on the assumption that neither Singapore nor anything else in that part of the world was worth fighting for so long as Nazi Germany had not been defeated. Yet the president could both embrace such a war plan and encourage his ambassador to Japan to follow a diplomatic posture diametrically opposed to it.

Roosevelt, however, did not care if his naval strategy and diplomatic policy were working at cross-purposes. When there was a topic with which he was intimately involved and interested he could take great pains to make sure that everything was just so. Such was the case in the Atlantic, where the president's oversight was meticulous. But Plan Dog and Rainbow 5 came from Stark and the Navy, not FDR. He could approve it just as he approved so many domestic programs emerging from one New Deal agency or another without worrying whether or not it was consistent with what the government was doing elsewhere. And his letter to Grew complimenting the ambassador for articulating his strong support of Singapore was not an FDR letter. It was drafted in the State Department by Stanley Hornbeck and sent to the White House for the president's signature. Just because he signed it did not mean he believed it. In fact, there were times when the president signed such letters without even reading them.[14] That Franklin Roosevelt did not wish to get caught up in bureaucratic infighting between the State Department and the Navy is understandable. But when they went in different directions it was the president's job to reconcile the conflicting policies.

In a domestic crisis for which no prior experience existed, such as the Great Depression, one might justify allowing different people to orchestrate conflicting attempts at solutions. But what justification is there for embracing a war plan that says Asia is unimportant and then supporting diplomats who say it is worth fighting to defend? In 1941, national defense policy was riding off in at least two directions at the same time.

If this portrayal of Roosevelt is correct—that is, if he was a president who had a penchant for making sharp deviations from the formally approved strategy and who was not interested in preparing plans that accorded to his strategic thought—then we should not be surprised about how he acted in July 1941. A new crisis emerged, this time with the German attack on the Soviet Union in June. As Soviet divisions retreated from Europe, Japan had the choice of attacking its hated rival to the north or taking advantage of Soviet preoccupation with Germany to move into the South Pacific and secure critical resources of oil from the Dutch East Indies. While always keeping the Soviet option open, Japan decided to move south. The Roosevelt administration responded with a cutoff of all trade with Japan. Now denied the one commodity without which it could not exist, oil, Japan had either to capitulate to American demands or seize the Dutch East Indies and take the oil it needed. The diplomatic stalemate that had dragged on since 1937 could not continue much longer. Assuming that Japan would opt for a push into the South Pacific rather than capitulate to the United States, President Roosevelt ordered the War Department to build up the Philippines as a block to Japanese expansion.

There are at least two ways to judge Roosevelt's actions in this situation. One is argued by Waldo Heinrichs and is quite persuasive. In effect, Heinrichs argues, the German attack on the Soviet Union gave Roosevelt an opportunity to tie up the German war machine if Soviet resistance could be maintained. Anything the

United States could do to that end would pay remarkable dividends in the European theater. One thing the United States could do was to make sure that Japan did not have a free hand to use against the Soviets. In this interpretation, it was not so much Southeast Asia or the South Pacific that motivated Roosevelt as it was support for the Soviet Union.[15] In such an interpretation, the president had not reversed course once again, but had simply applied existing strategy to a new situation that had emerged suddenly. On the other hand, there is substantial evidence that what moved Roosevelt was a desire to keep Japan out of the oil-rich Indies or to prevent it from sweeping through the South Seas and eventually linking up with Germany via the Suez Canal should it fall to German armies.

If Roosevelt was motivated by a desire to protect the South Pacific from Japanese attack, then his response to Japan's decision to head south in the summer of 1941 was a clear departure from the war plan he had approved. If he was worried that Japan might move south and link up with the Germans via Suez, he was Europe-oriented but still breaking from Rainbow 5. And even if he was thinking of making it unsafe for Japan to move north against the Soviet Union, Roosevelt was proclaiming a strategy for which there had been no previous planning. As we have seen again, the president was totally at ease in putting forward a strategy without any prior consultation with those who would have to implement it.

With the Navy preoccupied in the Atlantic, President Roosevelt instructed the Army to hold on to the Philippines. Faced with an impossible situation, the Army came up with a new weapon, the B-17 high-altitude bomber. This plane had proven remarkably effective in recent tests and the Army believed what it had to believe, that this technological breakthrough had changed the balance of power in the Pacific. At least it would change that balance once sufficient aircraft had been sent to the Philippines, the proper runways constructed there, and sufficient antiaircraft batteries installed. That would take time, more time than it appeared the Japanese were prepared to allow.

Here again, the president was faced with a serious gap between the strategy he had approved and the reality of American means to carry it out. On the one hand, the policy was to abandon Southeast Asia and the South Seas as expendable, and to that end naval forces had increasingly been concentrated in the Atlantic. On the other hand, the policy was to defend that region, and to that end the Army was building its defenses in the Philippines and establishing American airpower there. But if that was going to work, Roosevelt had to buy some time. That time could only come with some decisive presidential leadership within the national security establishment.

Franklin Roosevelt did not provide that. He did contemplate a summit conference with the Japanese premier but was talked out of the idea by Secretary Hull. A dramatic proposal for reordering Japanese-American relations did make the rounds of the national security staff late in 1941 but that emerged from lower-level bureaucrats and the president paid no attention to it as the national security establishment cut it to shreds.

Perhaps there was nothing the president could have done to have bought the time necessary to build up defenses in the Philippines. As events played out, however, war came before American forces in Asia were prepared and the consequences were disastrous; graphic evidence of what can happen if a nation pursues a strategic policy without the means to carry it out.

What this last situation illustrates is the Roosevelt presidential style that did little to reconcile ends and means of strategic plans. At other times the president thought up new strategies but failed to tell anyone about them so they could be planned. And he allowed different branches of his national security structure to work at cross-purposes. Indeed, he encouraged it.

Sometimes this managerial style was irrelevant to the course of events as no crisis existed. At other times he was in the middle of a crisis. Whether greater coordination and control over strategic planning would have altered the course of events appreciably is a different and much more difficult question to answer than the one this essay addresses. Here, I have sought to examine how the president managed strategic policy issues, to understand his style. I conclude that in national security matters as in domestic matters, the president's style was to allow anarchy to reign and to call it a plan.

NOTES

1. Russell Buhite and David W. Levy, eds., *FDR's Fireside Chats* (Norman: Univ. of Oklahoma Press, 1992), 21; Minutes of the Dec. 11, 1934, meeting of the National Emergency Council in Lester G. Seligman and Elmer E. Cornwall, Jr., eds., *New Deal Mosaic: Roosevelt Confers with His National Emergency Council, 1933-1936.* (Eugene: Univ. of Oregon Books, 1965), 365.
2. Waldo Heinrichs, "Role of the U.S. Navy," in *Pearl Harbor as History: Japanese-American Relations, 1931-1941,* ed., Dorothy Borg and Shumpei Okamoto (New York: Columbia Univ. Press, 1973), 209.
3. The importance of naval and air bases to American war plans shifted during the 1930s. For a discussion of these matters see Edward S. Miller, *War Plan Orange: The U.S. Strategy to Defeat Japan, 1897-1945* (Annapolis: Naval Institute Press, 1991).
4. Miller, *War Plan Orange,* 11.
5. For an examination of the issues surrounding the Quarantine Speech and a list of the primary sources relating to it, see Jonathan G. Utley, *Going to War with Japan, 1937-1941* (Knoxville: Univ. of Tennessee Press, 1985), 16-22; Dorothy Borg, *The United States and the Far Eastern Crisis, 1933 1938* (Cambridge: Harvard Univ. Press, 1964), chap. 13; John McVicker Haight, "Roosevelt and the Aftermath of the Quarantine Speech," *Review of Politics* 24 (1962): 233-59.
6. Arthur Sweetzer, memo of conversation with Roosevelt, May 29, 1942, Arthur Sweetzer Papers, Library of Congress, Washington, D.C.
7. On Roosevelt and use of naval power, see Harold L. Ickes, *The Secret Diary of Harold L. Ickes* (New York: Simon and Schuster, 1954), 2:274; Henry Morgenthau, Jr. Diary, Franklin D. Roosevelt Library, Hyde Park, N.Y., 103:59ff; Bradford A. Lee, *Britain and the Sino-Japanese War, 1937-1939* (Stanford, Cal.: Stanford Univ. Press, 1973), 89-90; James R. Leutze, *Bargaining for Supremacy: Anglo-American Naval Relations, 1937-1941* (Chapel Hill: Univ. of North Carolina Press, 1977), 17-28; Borg, *Crisis,* 510-12; Alexander Cadogan, *The Diaries of Sir Alexander Cadogan* (New York: Putnam, 1972), 33-40; Sumner Welles memos, Jan. 8, 13, 1938, U.S. Department of State, *Papers Relating to the Foreign Relations of the United States, 1938* (Washington: Government Printing Office [GPO], 1954), 3:7-8, 19.

8. Joseph C. Grew diary, 127:4083, 4127, Houghton Library, Harvard University.
9. For a summary of the disagreement about moving the fleet to Pearl Harbor, see James O. Richardson, *On the Treadmill to Pearl Harbor* (Washington: GPO, 1972), 424-30.
10. Utley, *Going to War With Japan,* 88-89.
11. Waldo Heinrichs, *Threshold of War: Franklin D. Roosevelt and American Entry into World War II* (New York: Oxford Univ. Press, 1988).
12. On the development of Plan Dog, see Tracy Kittredge, "United States British Naval Relations, 1939-1942," typescript, ComNavEu file, Operational Archives, Washington, D.C.; Heinrichs, *Threshold of War,* 38; Miller, *War Plan Orange,* 269-70.
13. David Reynolds, *The Creation of the Anglo-American Alliance, 1937-1941* (Chapel Hill: Univ. of North Carolina Press, 1982), 182-85; Utley, *Going to War with Japan,* 114-15.
14. The thesis that Roosevelt did not always pay attention to or agree with what he approved is considered in Utley, *Going to War with Japan,* passim. This particular incident is discussed at 115-16.
15. See Heinrichs, *Threshold of War,* 144-45, and Waldo Heinrichs, "The Russian Factor," in *Diplomacy and Force: America's Road to War, 1931-1941,* ed. Marc Gallicchio and Jonathan Utley (Chicago: Imprint Publications, 1996).

SIX

THE EVOLUTION OF THE U.S. FLEET, 1933-1941: HOW THE PRESIDENT MATTERED

Thomas C. Hone

Introduction

SEVERAL DEVELOPMENTS can be identified as key elements in the victories of the United States Fleet in its Atlantic and Pacific campaigns during World War II. In the Atlantic struggle, the following were the keys to success: (1) code breaking and high-frequency direction finding (HFDF); (2) the ability of shipyards in the United States to produce enough merchant ships and armed escorts, especially destroyer escorts; (3) the successful application of land- and carrier-based aviation to antisubmarine warfare (ASW); and (4) the development and then the fielding of both radar and sonar. In the Pacific, there were seven key factors: (1) the creation and then the effective use of a large carrier-based air force combined with a force of underway replenishment ships; (2) the effective use of submarines against Japanese shipping; (3) amphibious warfare; (4) the successful application of radar to antiair and antisurface combat; (5) code breaking; (6) the ability to engage in battle while sensing the battle space through electronic indicators—radar and sonar screens; and (7) the ability to plan and then execute complex, far-flung operations in a relatively short period of time.

At issue is whether Franklin D. Roosevelt assisted the United States Navy in developing these critical technologies and techniques. How much did he, as constitutional commander in chief, matter? Basic to this question is another: What means were available to him, as president, if he wished to matter? The second question is a prelude to the first. If the president could not influence the fleet in ways that would promote its military success, then how could he claim responsibility for its victories—or, for that matter, be blamed for its defeats?

Put another way, how could the president set the stage for victory *without* trying to manage the Navy himself? As Wayne Hughes of the Naval Postgraduate School has observed, "the president as commander-in-chief mainly creates an environment." A president does so primarily in three ways. First, by deciding, with Congress, how the government's money is to be spent. Second, by selecting his subordinates—the leaders of the nation's military forces. Third, by setting the national security goals of the nation; in particular, by guiding the nation's foreign policy.[1] These are basic standards against which to judge Roosevelt's actions. What did he do? And, what were the consequences of his decisions, especially in these three areas?

Scholars have described in detail Roosevelt's interest in the Navy, his actions to shape the nature of the fleet, and his use of his formal powers to place certain admirals in the Navy's top positions. Based on their work, I shall argue that—as president—Roosevelt "was frequently guilty of dabbling in his hobby, the Navy, but his grand instinct . . . was correct, as was the overall course he charted for the Navy."[2] We have all read Roosevelt's lament: ". . . the Treasury and the State Department put together are nothing compared with the Na-a-vy. . . . To change anything in the Na-a-vy is like punching a feather bed. You punch it with your right and you punch it with your left until you are finally exhausted, and then you find the damn bed just as it was before you started punching."[3] If he was in fact successful in preparing the Navy for war, why the frustration? Was he deliberately exaggerating? The answer, I think, is "no." He was not necessarily exaggerating. But his frustration was as much with his role as commander in chief as it was with the Navy itself. After 1933, Roosevelt's influence over the Navy was great, yet Roosevelt understood better than most the limits on his formal, constitutional powers and on his informal influence. He knew he had to combine initiative and restraint. The rest of the paper will show how he did that.

The Innovations that Won the Naval War

Work done on intercepting and then deciphering and translating enemy radio messages was critical to the military success of the Allies in World War II, particularly in the Atlantic and Pacific naval campaigns. In the U.S. Navy, this work began as a small-scale effort and gradually grew in scope and importance as radio reception equipment improved and the value of the information gained through interception and decryption was appreciated.[4] As one of the leaders of Navy cryptologic efforts put it in 1937, "whereas before 1930 we were able to keep abreast of changes with 2 cryptanalysts and 2 clerks, we are not fully able to do so now with 8 times the force and a lot of complicated machinery."[5]

At the same time, the importance of high-frequency direction finding also grew. In Fleet Problem XV (May 1934), for example, the radio intelligence unit in battleship *Mississippi* found the main "enemy" formation through the use of HFDF. The next year, in Fleet Problem XVI, both "sides" located "enemy" submarines after the submarines transmitted radio messages while surfaced. And in Fleet Problem XX (1939), communications intelligence personnel on carrier *Ranger* discovered "enemy" carrier *Enterprise* through the use of HFDF, allowing *Ranger's* aircraft to stage a successful surprise attack against her.[6] With the elevation of Admiral J. M. Reeves to the post of Commander in Chief, United States Fleet, in 1934, Navy interest in communications intelligence grew. By 1936, for Fleet Problem XVII, the Navy Department, at the insistence of the chief of naval operations, did not allow newspaper correspondents or photographers to accompany the ships that participated. This was done to conceal new HFDF equipment and the reliance upon communications intelligence by command staffs.[7]

Once war began, the Navy's communications intelligence community faced two very serious problems. The first was how to reorganize to deal with a veritable flood of transmissions and the new personnel required to deal with them. The second, described with candor by W. J. Holmes in his *Double-Edged Secrets,* was how best to use the information gained from interceptions and decryptions.[8] The result was, first, the creation of ad hoc procedures and organizations—described by Holmes—and then, as the war progressed, the creation of an *industry* of communications intelligence and the alliance of that industry with other agencies that gathered and interpreted the many varieties of intelligence information. This industrialization of intelligence generally, and communications intelligence in particular, was a revolutionary event, as well as one of the great Allied feats of the war. Navy communications intelligence specialists, however, often resisted this revolution—this change of what had been the craft of artisans into a process of mass production. The prewar emphasis on intense secrecy and on the "magic" of encryption and decryption were difficult to overcome.

Carrier aviation was well established by the time the war began. As the Commander Aircraft, Battle Force, put it in a memo to the commander in chief of the United States Fleet in June 1937, *"Once an enemy carrier is within striking distance of our fleet no security remains until it—its squadrons—or both, are destroyed"*(emphasis in the original).[9] However, what was not established at all, prewar, was the contribution a *fleet* of carriers, sustained by a mobile replenishment force, could make to a U.S. Navy offensive against Japan's Imperial Navy. Not even the Navy's leading aviators grasped this.

The Japanese and United States strategies in a Pacific war were clear to both sides before the war began. Japanese forces would try to secure a double ring of defenses against the offensive assault of the United States. Using interior lines of communication and long-range aircraft, the Japanese military leaders hoped to hold off and blunt attacks, thereby wearing down the willingness of the population of the United States to accept a long war of attrition. The combination of massed carriers, carrying hundreds of strike aircraft, with underway refueling and replenishment ships, trumped the Japanese strategy. It was the Japanese who counted on holding the strategic initiative. The combined carrier/replenishment force took that initiative away from them.

This was a real change from the prewar concept of the carrier and its aircraft as a strike weapon of limited endurance. Prewar exercises had emphasized scenarios where carriers and their aircraft were expended or lost early in a conflict. Carrier aircraft had great potential for scouting and—by the late 1930s, when ordnance loads increased—for strike. But as one carrier commander noted in 1937, "carriers cannot provide their own protection against enemy aircraft attack during the two critical periods [dawn and dusk] when such attacks are most to be expected."[10] Carrier battles were expected to proceed like those at Midway in June 1942: the first side to find and attack the other would usually gain the victory. Carriers were necessary, and their aircraft, deployed promptly, could exterminate enemy carriers, but the impact of carriers on a naval campaign was expected to be immediate and of limited duration. Again, the prewar exercises suggested a Midway scenario. The carriers would decimate one another and most of their aircraft would be lost. The battle would continue only if both sides had surface units, submarines, and land-based aircraft to throw in. If one side emerged from the carrier fight with most of its carriers intact, it would win the battle but not necessarily the campaign because there was no way to sustain a large force of carriers at sea to take advantage of the initial victory.

Prewar, carriers were masters of the tactical ambush and raid. What the U.S. Navy needed to defeat the Japanese strategy of defense during the war, however, was a force capable of taking and holding the strategic initiative. Then, the U.S. Navy would set the tempo and determine the direction of the war. Of all the factors that would give the U.S. Navy a carrier air force with strategic effect, two stand out. The first was underway replenishment. As Thomas Wildenberg has noted, the foundations for underway replenishment were laid in 1939 but not implemented fully until 1943.[11] The delay was largely due to the need of the Navy to wait for the production of high-speed tankers procured through the Maritime Commission.[12] The second factor was carrier defense. It made no sense to employ large numbers of carriers as an offensive striking force if they could not be defended. As Clark Reynolds observed in his classic *The Fast Carriers,* there was no "standardized Pacific Fleet fighter direction doctrine" even by September 1943.[13]

Effective air defense of carriers depended upon a merging of technology with doctrine. The technology consisted of Information, Friend or Foe (IFF) transponders, an effective air search radar with a Plan Position Indicator (PPI) scope, and multichannel very high frequency (VHF) radios that allowed ship-based fighter directors to direct defensive fighters against incoming waves of enemy attack aircraft.[14] The doctrine was that "surface ships must be integrated and coordinated with naval air forces, rather than the reverse."[15] That is, the key to carrier defense was coordination of all air defense assets (fighters, antiaircraft guns) by aviators working from a special air defense center on an aircraft carrier. Put another way, there was an air defense system, with several layers, centered on and controlled by the carriers themselves. Once this system was working, then carriers could combine it with their great strategic mobility (a function of the mobile service squadrons of oilers and replenishment ships) to isolate and then destroy key elements of the Japanese defenses *before* the Japanese could take advantage of their interior lines of communication.

Antisubmarine warfare (ASW) was another area in which the U.S. Navy's prewar experience and doctrine was inadequate for the wartime challenge. The basic strategic problem was that the Navy did not begin preparing for a two-ocean war until it was almost too late, so that, when war came, there were not enough escorts and ASW patrol aircraft to go around. This shortage of equipment affected both the Atlantic and Pacific campaigns. The former case is better known. In late December 1941, for example, the commander of the Eastern Sea Frontier, Admiral Adolphus Andrews, told the chief of naval operations that "should enemy submarines operate off this coast, this Command has no forces available to take adequate action against them."[16] However, ships were almost as scarce in the Pacific. From December 27, 1941, through June 30, 1942, for example, of 54 convoys from West Coast ports to Alaska and back, 44 were escorted by only one destroyer or destroyer minesweeper.[17] The Imperial Japanese Navy had a force of long-range submarines. Had they employed them early in the war along the Pacific coast of North America, as the German navy did its submarines along the Atlantic coast, the consequences could have been catastrophic for the U.S. Navy.

Yet as Eliot Cohen and John Gooch pointed out in their *Military Misfortunes,* the problem with U.S. Navy ASW efforts early in the war was not just a shortage of ships, aircraft, and trained personnel. It was in the way the Navy had prepared organizationally for war. As Cohen and Gooch argued, "*the navy's leadership defined its problem as that of acquiring technical information, not assimilating new forms of organization*" (emphasis in the original).[18] The prewar fleet problems had concentrated on the war in the Pacific, and on the use of submarines in that war to shadow and then to attack main fleet units. The mission of convoy protection was not emphasized, and the task of escorting surface ships was basically perceived as one for the local commanders to solve. As Cohen and Gooch pointed out, however, the Royal Navy had already learned that ASW was essentially a war of information. The U.S. Navy's observers who consulted with their Royal Navy counterparts before the United States formally entered the war saw this but failed to understand what they were seeing and how to copy it.

There is another factor: the problem the U.S. Navy had of placing ASW and antiair commands on land and linking them to fleet units. The first time any commandant of a naval district had operational control of long-distance HFDF equipment was in Fleet Problem XIX in 1938. And, even in that case, only two of the three naval district headquarters involved had what was referred to as "net control," or the ability to issue high priority "flash" messages to the operating forces under their command.[19] As Cohen and Gooch well understood, the key question facing the U.S. Navy in its ASW campaign against U-boats in 1942 was, "How quickly could the Navy's leaders learn?" The evidence from the Navy's fleet problems suggests that some "good" (and, alas, much more "bad") learning had already taken place. Why the lessons of Fleet Problem XIX were apparently lost is not clear.

The reverse side of this coin was the initial poor showing of U.S. Navy submarines against Japanese merchant ships, despite the fact that the U.S. Navy announced a campaign of unrestricted submarine warfare against the Japanese fleet and merchant navy the day after war was declared. Some of this was due to faulty torpedoes—more specifically to detonators that did not work as intended.[20] But more was due to shortsighted tactical training. Prewar exercises had emphasized attacks against the enemy fleet, which meant cautious approaches in daylight using sound gear. As one officer involved in U.S. Navy Fleet Problem XIX (1938) noted, "submarines in smooth water [must] conduct their attacks from deep submergence using sound equipment."[21] This emphasis on a conservative approach to battle was not easy to overcome, as Clay Blair documented in his *Silent Victory: The U.S. Submarine War against Japan.*[22] Combined with the faulty torpedoes, the need to retrain Navy submarine commanders (and in many cases to remove them from operational command) delayed the Navy's campaign against Japanese merchant shipping by about a year.

Radar and sonar were both naval developments. In the years between World Wars I and II, the Naval Research Laboratory went beyond the lower-frequency sound-ranging and detection equipment used in 1918 and developed supersonic active and passive sonars. The laboratory also pioneered radar development, building a pulse radar in 1934 and demonstrating a prototype air search radar in 1936.[23] The latter promised a revolution in naval warfare. By the fall of 1937, for example, the Fleet Training Division in the Office of the Chief of Naval Operations thought that the combination of "radioecho range detection" and the 6-inch, 47 caliber gun would serve as an effective shield against aircraft attacking from higher altitudes, including dive bombers *before* they reached their dive points.[24] As it happened, radar contributed more to the direction of carrier-based fighter defense. If the link between the 6-inch gun (using proximity-fused ammunition) and radar had been established by 1941, defense of carriers might well have stayed where it was prewar—in the hands of surface ship officers. Aircraft themselves might also have been much less effective in their attacks on surface forces.[25]

As Norman Friedman has shown in his *U.S. Naval Weapons,* the Navy's Bureau of Ordnance carried on an active program of research in the years before World War II.[26] The bureau developed the very effective 5-inch, 38 caliber gun, which, when coupled with effective fire control(also developed under the bureau's supervision), was a potent weapon against air and surface targets. Ordnance also developed two 16-inch guns, a 12-inch gun, an 8-inch, 55 caliber gun for heavy cruisers, and a fast-firing 6-inch, 47 caliber gun for light cruisers. The bureau also cooperated with the Massachusetts Institute of Technology (MIT) in pioneering servomechanisms to link range finders with the guns they controlled. Finally, the bureau also supported the development of the proximity fuse in time for that innovation to play a significant role in antiaircraft gunnery during the war.[27] As a result of these (and related) efforts, the U.S. Navy possessed excellent ordnance (except torpedoes) and fire control equipment when Japanese forces attacked.

Unfortunately, many Navy personnel who needed it had not experienced sufficient training with this equipment when war began. This was one very important reason why surface force commanders were having problems using radar to direct their forces in the battles around Guadalcanal in 1942. In addition, the technology of radar detection was installed on ships before the technology of what came to be called the "combat information center" (CIC)—and CIC was needed to control and effectively use radar. The Naval Research Laboratory also did not develop an airborne radar before the war. The cavity magnetron, the key device behind microwave radar, was a British innovation. Finally, uniformed Navy leaders, particularly Vice Admiral Harold G. Bowen, himself a former innovative head of the Navy's Bureau of Engineering, apparently did not "hit it off" with the scientists of the National Defense Research Committee (NDRC, formed in June 1940), especially the NDRC's first leader, scientist Vannevar Bush. Though Vice Admiral Bowen had already (in 1939) supported Naval Research Laboratory study of the utility of nuclear-power propulsion for nuclear submarines, Harvey Sapolsky has argued that Bowen's poor relations with Bush and other scientists was the reason why Bush decided to shift the locus of much military research and development from agencies such as the Naval Research Laboratory to university laboratories, such as MIT's.[28]

Developing the doctrine and tools of amphibious warfare began in November and December 1933, when the Marine Corps started work on what became its "Tentative Manual for Landing Operations" and when (in December) the Fleet Marine Force was created.[29] But both the Navy and the Marine Corps lacked the resources necessary for full-scale amphibious operations. The Fleet

Marine Force was also quite small—only 74 officers and 1,177 enlisted personnel in the spring of 1934.[30] This force was starved for basic types of equipment. It lacked adequate landing craft, amphibious tractors and tanks, and aircraft. Even without the necessary equipment, however, exercises advanced doctrine to the point that, in 1938, Marine Corps representatives could tell the Navy's General Board that the difference between success and failure in storming a defended beach was the length of the interval in which there would be no gunfire or air support for assault troops.[31] But there were some concepts that could not be tested without the proper equipment or without the funds for large-scale exercises. Gunfire support from ships offshore was never adequate before the war, and the command and control of amphibious operations was primitive.[32]

Merchant ship construction was a different story. Congress had established a program to subsidize commercial shipping firms in the Merchant Marine Act of 1928. The firms could—and did—use the federal payments for mail delivery to enlarge and modernize their fleets. In 1934, the Shipping Board Bureau of the Department of Commerce began development of standardized merchant ship designs that the Navy could adapt to wartime use. In 1936, Congress eliminated the Shipping Board and created in its place the Maritime Commission. The latter paid shipbuilders the difference between their actual costs and the prices charged by foreign competitors for similar ships *if* the U.S. shipbuilders agreed to construct ships to Maritime Commission standards. "The Maritime Commission itself was staffed largely by former Navy civilian employees; its first chief was the former head of the Navy's Bureau of Construction and Repair. In addition, all contract plans and specifications for ships being built under subsidy were cleared first by the Navy Department."[33] The work of the commission was critical to providing the Navy with high-speed tankers and other standard designs that could be converted to auxiliaries (such as destroyer and seaplane tenders) when war threatened.

The commission was also instrumental in preparing the ship-building industry for the great production surge required to overcome the U-boat threat in the Atlantic. In December 1940, for example, private shipbuilders in the United States were scheduled to complete approximately 700,000 cargo-tons of ships in 1942. That target was boosted by the Maritime Commission in March 1941 to over 3 million cargo tons—and then again on December 1, 1941, to 6 million cargo tons. The industry met the higher figure, surging production in 1943, the critical year of the Atlantic U-boat campaign. This performance was superior to that during World War I, when the American shipbuilders had reached their peak output *after* the war had ended, in 1919.[34]

Finally, the Navy had developed, by the late 1930s, a cadre of officers able to plan and then direct a huge force over a great theater of war. Starting in 1928-1929, Naval War College classes of higher-ranking officers (commanders and captains) focused "on the strategic, logistical, and tactical elements for [an] advance west-ward across the Pacific, which required taking advance bases to support the fleet."[35] By 1936, Captain Raymond A. Spruance and his fellow faculty members had tailored the so-called advanced course at the college for officers who would, if war came, be responsible for the work of planning trans-Pacific operations.[36] Their efforts paralleled work being done in the War Plans Division of the Office of the Chief of Naval Operations[37] and in the fleet, where future strategic planners such as Charles M. Cooke, Jr., Forrest P. Sherman, and Harry W. Hill served on the staffs of fleet commanders such as Claude C. Bloch.[38] This confluence of the work of three institutions—the Naval War College, the War Plans Division, and the fleet planning staff—prepared a cluster of officers for positions of planning and orchestrating a great campaign. Edward Miller, author of *War Plan Orange,* regards this maturing of Navy commanders and their staff deputies as one of the most important reasons for the defeat of Japan. The Navy had skilled planners who could use the huge material resources at their disposal by 1944 to grasp and then retain the strategic initiative in the Pacific war.

President Roosevelt as Resource Manager

When Roosevelt took office, the Navy was at a low point in terms of resources. The initial reaction of his administration was *to cut Navy spending even more*. On April 10, 1933, Secretary of the Navy Claude Swanson sent a memo to "All Bureaus and Offices" warning them that expenditures would be reduced in fiscal year 1934 (starting in July 1933).[39] But then Roosevelt changed his mind. Instead of focusing on reducing the nation's debt by slashing federal expenditures, he set the debt issue aside and opted for using federal spending to boost demand. From the Navy's perspective, his most important initiative—as described in detail by Robert H. Levine in his *The Politics of American Naval Rearmament, 1930-1938*—was to persuade Congress to accept the notion that shipbuilding was a form of public works. This allowed Roosevelt to channel money earmarked for industrial recovery to the construction of warships. The president, assisted by Navy Secretary Swanson, was also able to persuade Congress to increase spending on the Navy generally, so that the Navy could tackle the backlog of maintenance and repair that had built up during the Hoover administration.

Spending on all Navy ships in commission in 1922, for example, had totaled $192,406,786 for that fiscal year. Through the 1920s and early 1930s, the comparable figures were less than 80 percent of that for 1922. Only in 1933 did money spent on fleet maintenance and operation begin to approach the total for 1922; only in 1939 did such spending exceed that for 1922.[40] The problem of low spending for operations and maintenance had become severe in the Hoover administration because of the rapid growth of naval aviation. In August 1926, for example, the Navy had 8 operational aircraft squadrons. That number increased to 27 in June 1928 and to 32 at the beginning of 1933.[41] Yet spending for operations and maintenance had been held roughly constant during that time. With the need expanding and the resources kept fixed, something had to give—and it was the general readiness of the fleet. The Roosevelt administration acted, with the support and encouragement of Carl Vinson, chairman of the Naval Affairs Committee of the House of Representatives, to alleviate this problem.

At the same time, however, Roosevelt, Swanson, and Vinson cooperated to persuade first the Bureau of the Budget and then the Congress to accept the idea that the latter should give the Navy a blanket authorization to build enough new ships to bring the fleet to the force levels allowed by the Washington Treaty for the Limitation of Armament of 1922.[42] Efforts to pass such authorizing legislation (in 1930 and again in 1932) during the Hoover administration had failed. In 1930, the argument against a blanket authorization was that the London Conference called to reconsider the Washington Treaty might actually reduce the latter's tonnage allowances. In 1932, the authorization was turned down because the Congress, though controlled by the Democrats (in the House only), was still not committed to *increasing* federal expenditures as a means of dealing with the economic depression.[43]

The use of National Industrial Recovery Act (NIRA) funds for ship construction in 1933 (for 2 aircraft carriers, 2 heavy cruisers, 4 light cruisers, 21 destroyers, and 4 submarines) was a temporary, emergency measure. The blanket authorization to bring the Navy to "treaty strength" was the Naval Parity (or Vinson-Trammell) Act of March 1934. Though it was a step forward for the process of naval rearmament, it did not open the floodgates. Even though the president's party controlled both the Senate and the House after 1932, key committee positions were in the hands of conservative legislators—particularly James Byrnes, who chaired the naval subcommittee of the Senate Appropriations Committee—who were not strong supporters of a large Navy.[44] There were also numerous and vocal advocates of neutrality in Congress, and congressional hearings on the role of the arms industry in instigating World War I began in 1934. But the concept of a steady buildup of the fleet, based on a long-range plan—a concept championed by two successive chiefs of naval operations (CNO), William V. Pratt (1930-1933) and William H. Standley (1933-1937)—was made law in 1934, and that law served as the basis for American naval rearmament.

The development of a balanced "treaty fleet" took time, however. In the summer of 1934, the president summoned the fleet to New York for a formal review. Most of the Navy that he and his fellow citizens viewed was a force created or sustained by his predecessors. All of the battleships, for example, were either in commission or being built when Roosevelt was himself assistant secretary of the Navy under Secretary Josephus Daniels. The same ·vas true for the light (or scout) cruisers of the *Omaha* type and for the destroyers and fleet auxiliaries. The newer ships, including carriers *Lexington, Saratoga,* and *Ranger* and heavy cruisers of the *Pensacola* and *Northampton* types, were the product of previous Republican administrations, as was the great airship *Macon*. The "treaty fleet" gained strength slowly. In fiscal year 1934, 4 heavy cruisers of a new and stronger type (*Astoria's*) and 1 new destroyer were commissioned; in fiscal year 1935, 1 heavy cruiser and 6 new destroyers; in 1936, another heavy cruiser, 2 destroyer leaders, and 4 submarines. In 1937, "Roosevelt's navy" began to emerge, with yet another heavy cruiser, 24 destroyers, 2 gunboats (*Erie* and *Charleston,* heavily armed ships favored by former CNO Pratt), and 6 submarines. In fiscal year 1938, carriers *Enterprise* and *Yorktown,* both financed by the NIRA allotments of 1933, were commissioned, along with 5 light cruisers (*Brooklyn's*), 12 destroyers, and 6 additional submarines. Fiscal year 1939 brought 1 heavy cruiser (*Wichita*), 3 light cruisers, 8 destroyers, 4 submarines, 2 minesweepers, 1 cargo ship, and 1 fleet tug.[45]

Roosevelt deliberately promoted his image as a "Navy man," but the Navy did not really grow beyond treaty limits until well into his second administration, with the passage of the Naval Expansion Act of May 1938. Influenced then by the crisis in Europe, Congress authorized increases of 40,000 tons of aircraft carriers, 135,000 tons of battleships, over 68,000 tons of cruisers, and an increase in the number of first-line naval aircraft to 3,000. The real breakthrough came only in June 1940, after the fall of France, when Congress first increased aircraft carrier tonnage by another 79,500 tons (on June 14), then added to it another 200,000 tons on July 19. The number of Navy aircraft was increased to 4,500 on June 14, to 10,000 the next day, and then to a total of 15,000 on July 19.

This was a dramatic contrast with the mid-1930s, however, when the administration and Congress forced the Navy's civilian and military leaders to carefully justify every dollar and every sailor requested. Personnel growth actually lagged behind the increase in the number of ships. There were approximately 5,900 officers and 79,700 enlisted men in the Navy in 1933, and only 6,800 officers and 110,000 enlisted men in 1939.[46] These were increases of about 15 and 27 percent, respectively. But the number of combatant ships increased more over the same period—40 percent for carriers and heavy and light cruisers, and much more than that for modern destroyers, where the number jumped from 4 in commission in 1934 to 63 in 1939.[47] It should not come as any surprise that even the first-line fleet units, such as the carriers, newer battleships, and heavy cruisers, were manned at 90 percent of the *peacetime* allotment in 1939, while lesser units (older destroyers and submarines, especially) were manned at levels of 75 percent or less.[48]

Nevertheless, the fleet in 1939 was "balanced" in a way it had not been in 1933. New battleships had been authorized, with higher cruising speeds (27-28 knots), 16-inch guns, and new fire control equipment. There were several dozen new heavy and light cruisers, new carriers *Yorktown* and *Enterprise* (with *Wasp* on the way), over 60 new destroyers, and almost 30 new submarines. Though constrained in terms of quantity and quality by treaty, by a lack of funds, and by pacifist concerns expressed in Congress, the *modern* Navy was finally taking shape. There was still only one major weakness in that Navy: auxiliaries, from fast tankers to seaplane tenders, from seagoing tugs to troopships and landing barges for the marines. As Thomas Wildenberg has shown, Chief of Naval Operations Admiral William H. Standley did his best to persuade the Navy's General Board and President Roosevelt to pursue a regular program of auxiliary construction in 1934 and 1935. Though assisted by arguments from Admiral Joseph M. Reeves, commander in chief of the United States Fleet, and Secretary of the Navy Swanson, Standley could not budge the president and Congress. Only when his friend Admiral William D. Leahy became chief of naval operations in 1937 did Roosevelt support a long-term program for the construction of fleet auxiliaries, and even then the president's support was tepid.[49]

Finally, as resource manager, Roosevelt had to work within—and was therefore constrained by—the patterns of executive-branch management that his Republican predecessors had persuaded Congress to create in the 1920s. For example, the chief of naval operations prepared a report for the secretary of the Navy describing his proposals for legislation in a given fiscal year about *15 months* before that year began. In other words, the CNO and his staff had in hand such a report in the spring of 1934 for the fiscal year 1936, which actually began in July 1935. But this report was based upon prior studies done and hearings conducted by the General Board, and upon recommendations by the Navy's bureaus. If the president wanted to direct this process, it was best that he intervene early, before all the studies were done and before the CNO had made his recommendations to the secretary of the Navy.

This is why CNO Pratt's work on a long-term, steady building program—work rejected by President Hoover in 1932—was critical in the spring of 1933, when Roosevelt decided to abandon his presidential campaign platform (calling for further cuts in federal expenditures) and ask Congress for permission to use National Industrial Recovery Act funds for Navy ship construction.

Roosevelt did not have his own naval building program in June 1933 (though he was clearly critical of Hoover's). He had to rely on the outgoing chief of naval operations and on recommendations made by the new secretary of the Navy (who was in turn influenced by the members of the General Board) and Carl Vinson, chairman of the House Naval Affairs Committee. It was only in 1934 that Roosevelt could begin to get inside the Navy's formal budget procedure, and of course that meant his direct *budget* influence would not be felt until fiscal year 1936.

Roosevelt's Appointments

When Roosevelt took office, the uniformed leaders of the Navy were disheartened and divided. Admiral William V. Pratt, the chief of naval operations, had tried unsuccessfully to find a middle ground between the arms limitation policy of the Hoover administration and the desire of other senior officers (especially the members of the General Board) to modernize the fleet and bring it up to allowed treaty levels. Roosevelt, who had first met Pratt when the latter commanded battleship *New York* in 1919, asked the CNO to stay on temporarily (Pratt had been scheduled to retire in February 1933) to smooth the transition of presidential administrations. As Craig Symonds pointed out, "Admiral Pratt served four unhappy months under Franklin Roosevelt. His job remained what it had been under the Republicans: keeping the Navy as efficient as possible with the smallest possible amount of funding."[50]

Pratt's short tenure as a holdover CNO was clouded by Roosevelt's refusal to commit his administration to a long-term building and modernization program that Pratt had developed. As CNO, Pratt had taken seriously the initiatives of President Hoover to improve the efficiency of federal management. Pratt had argued to Hoover's secretary of the Navy, Charles Francis Adams, that one such initiative had to be the reorganization of the fleet so that the command authority of the commander in chief of the United States Fleet was clear and legally well defined.[51] Adams, and then Hoover, had accepted Pratt's arguments. But Pratt had no such good fortune with the new president, nor with new Secretary of the Navy Claude Swanson. The personal "chemistry" was not right. Roosevelt wanted someone else.

Pratt's replacement was Admiral William H. Standley, appointed in July 1933. Standley, unlike Pratt and Standley's own successor, Admiral William D. Leahy, had not personally known Franklin Roosevelt when the latter was assistant secretary of the Navy from 1913 to 1920. Perhaps as a result, "Standley was never on intimate terms with the president . . ." and "he did not enjoy the kind of camaraderie with Roosevelt that his successors did."[52] The admiral had other problems, as well: "Swanson was taken ill in early 1933, and was incapable of carrying out the full functions of his job for the rest of that year, part of 1934, and, again, virtually all of 1936."[53] To make matters worse, Standley's personal relationship with Swanson's assistant secretary was "poisonous," and "the president wanted to be his own secretary of the navy."[54]

Yet Standley stayed as CNO until January 1937, despite the fact that he was not a presidential intimate and despite his efforts to increase the administrative influence and formal authority of the Office of the Chief of Naval Operations—efforts Roosevelt rebuffed. Standley wanted to continue Pratt's work in improving the ways in which the Navy was controlled. Pratt had worked on the military side—on the chain of command from the fleet's commander in chief to the various main forces of the fleet. Standley took as his task the rationalizing of the shore command. Specifically, he wanted to give the office of the CNO authority over the bureaus.

When Standley became CNO, the bureau chiefs reported directly to the secretary of the Navy, as did the General Board, which recommended both ship designs and ship construction programs to the secretary. Standley, charged by law with preparing the Navy for war, could not control the Navy's organizations—its bureaus—which did the actual work (training, personnel actions, designing and purchasing ships, aircraft, and ammunition, etc.). To his frustration, the president would not allow him direct control over the bureaus.[55] As Roosevelt said in a letter to Swanson in March 1934, ". . . because the Secretary of the Navy is in the last analysis the official responsible to the President and the Congress . . . it is of the utmost importance that the Secretary of the Navy himself shall know what is going on every day in all major matters affecting all bureaus and offices."[56] There was another reason, too: the members of the Appropriations Committee of the House of Representatives wanted to be able to talk directly with the bureau chiefs when budget hearings were held.[57] Congress was not warm to the idea of a chief of naval operations who had the power to direct the work of the bureaus.

But Standley kept pressing. In September 1934, he directed "All Bureaus and Offices" to submit "All plans for new ship construction" to him before sending them to the secretary of the Navy for approval.[58] That same month, he argued to the eight bureau chiefs that a 1923 memorandum from the secretary of the Navy had given the CNO cognizance "of the progress of new construction." Under this authority, he "desired" the bureau chiefs to coordinate their separate but related activities "throughout the course of design, development, construction and procurement," and to tell his office when "conflicting interests of Bureaus cannot readily be reconciled."[59] If he could get the bureau chiefs to tell him when they disagreed, Standley knew he could act as referee and coordinator, thereby further increasing the influence of his office.

By the end of 1936, he had positioned the CNO at the center of three important internal Navy processes. The first was the writing of the "Annual Estimate of the Situation," which served as the basis for the budget estimates a year hence. That is, the "Annual Estimate" for the fiscal year 1938 (which began in July 1937) was written in the spring of 1936. This estimate was similar to the program objective memoranda (POMs) that the military services prepare today as part of the Planning, Programming, and Budgeting System (PPBS). The second process that Standley attempted (successfully) to influence was the preparation of the Annual Building Program. Once the sole preserve the General Board, the program, under Standley, passed through his hands before going on to the secretary of the Navy. Finally, Standley was able to gain limited influence over the budgeting process. Under the supervision of the assistant secretary of the Navy, the service's uniformed budget officer would hold annual confidential hearings with the bureau chiefs to reconcile bureau budget requests with anticipated allotments. Then the budget officer would recommend numbers to the CNO, and the CNO would meet with the bureau chiefs before budget requests were sent on to the assistant secretary of the Navy.[60] In effect, the CNO's office became, under Standley, central to all aspects of the "planning, programming, and budgeting" process.

Perhaps Standley's greatest success as an administrator was to make the War Plans Division of his office the clearinghouse for fleet plans, bureau proposals, and General Board studies. He was, as Edward S. Miller pointed out, the only prewar CNO who had also served as the director of the War Plans Division, and so Standley could perceive the possibility of using plans—and the doctrine derived from such plans—as tools for directing the development of the Navy as a whole. In 1933 and 1934, Standley and Captain S. W. Bryant (head of the War Plans Division), with the help of Admiral Joseph M. Reeves, soon to be named fleet commander in chief, initiated a "flourish of Pacific campaign planning."[61] This wave of planning, performed by about a dozen officers under Bryant's leadership, gave the Office of the Chief of Naval Operations greater status if not greater legal authority. It was Standley's only alternative, once Roosevelt had rejected his request for more legal authority over the bureaus.

The war planners could and did participate in hearings before the General Board, where trade-offs were made between types of forces (the battleline vs. task forces), ship characteristics (fire-power vs. endurance, for example), and even new technologies (which ships should have sonars, for example). Under Standley's leadership, the war planners in the CNO's office became the custodians of the only theater-level campaign plan that then existed, and they matched the proposals of the bureaus against that plan, objecting to deviations if and when they found them.

Despite his many contributions to Navy administration and naval policy, Standley left his post frustrated and tired.[62] Is it any wonder? The earlier Republican administrations had begun a process of making government administration more rational. Admiral Pratt had appealed to that model when he proposed reorganizing the fleet. Standley, however, found himself confronting a president who personally rejected the rational management model while publicly endorsing it, and this apparent contradiction puzzled and annoyed him. Roosevelt's concept of himself as chief executive did not include deferring to the chief of naval operations, and he hampered and obstructed Admiral Standley's effort to reform the highest levels of management within the Navy Department. Yet he kept Standley on. Why?

The answer, I think, is simple: Standley was a superb administrator. With Claude Swanson sick for two years of Standley's three-and-a-half year term in office, *someone* had to do the work, and do it well. Standley did, both in terms of policy (he sustained the fleet concept inherited from Pratt) and—more importantly—in terms of administrative reform. When he had had enough, he quit. In his place, Roosevelt appointed Admiral William D. Leahy, an officer who was both a friend and, later, a confidant.

Roosevelt had known Leahy (CNO from 1937 to 1939) and Leahy's successor, Admiral Harold R. Stark (CNO from 1939 to 1942) when the president was assistant Navy secretary in the Wilson administration and the admirals were younger officers. As Admiral Leahy recalled in his memoirs, Roosevelt "knew the history, details of the composition and of the operations of the United States Navy since its original establishment."[63] This store of knowledge was complemented, Leahy observed, by the chief executive's "amazing capacity to see the basic points of a problem and also to master a mass of detail."[64] The result was a very personal—even intimate—style of administration. With Admiral Leahy as CNO, the president could be very clever, indeed.

The frustrated effort of the Soviet Union to obtain naval material and ships in the United States illustrates the very subtle way Roosevelt, with the cooperation of Leahy, could use the Navy. In 1936, the Soviet government, through its New York–based Amtorg Trading Corporation and Carp Export and Import Corporation, had approached firms such as Bethlehem Steel in an effort to obtain armor plate for installation in cruisers and battleships.[65] The Soviet government had also asked for drawings and specifications of an aircraft carrier and several battleships, and had expressed an interest in purchasing a submarine from the Electric Boat Company. The firms referred the Amtorg and Carp representatives to the Navy Department, and so began a minor farce.

Secretary of the Navy Swanson told the representatives of the Soviet government that the Navy did not have the staff to furnish the plans for the carrier and the battleships, and the State Department informed them that the private firms would "be obliged to abide by such rules and regulations designed for the preservation of military secrets . . . as the competent authorities of this Government might find it necessary to prescribe."[66] That sent the Soviet representatives back to the Navy. Navy representatives, such as the chiefs of the Bureaus of Steam Engineering and Ordnance, told them that the Espionage Act of 1917 restricted what the Navy could offer in the way of technical help. This was not a lie. In 1935, the Bureau of Steam Engineering had stopped contract work with Parsons, the famous British turbine manufacturer, because that firm had released details of U.S. warship designs to other nations to which it supplied steam turbines.[67] In any case, said the Navy officers, the State Department had to issue export licenses for all such military equipment.

Back the Soviet representatives went to the State Department. State's Division of Eastern European Affairs worried that allowing the Soviet government to purchase 16-inch guns might violate the London Naval Agreement, which was about to be signed.[68] The day after the agreement was signed, the secretary of state wrote to Navy secretary Claude Swanson saying that an export license could be granted, but that any export of 16-inch guns would (a) threaten the desire of the United States government to hold the size of new battleship guns to 14-inches and (b) involve the Navy in the testing of the weapons, violating an established policy of "the Government to disassociate itself from the promotion of the export trade in such articles."[69]

The Russians went back to Bethlehem Shipbuilding Company, but Bethlehem could not get a clear statement of what was and was not legal from the Navy. A Bethlehem manager told the State Department's chief of the Office of Arms and Munitions Control in 1937 that Navy officers were stonewalling, and that the Office of Naval Intelligence (ONI) was releasing garbled reports of the proposed transaction to the press.[70] State checked with the Navy, and Admiral Leahy, the new chief of naval operations, said that Bethlehem did not want to sign a contract with the Russians because it could not make the equipment they wanted without the Navy's technical assistance, and such "active and prolonged cooperation in the manufacture of battleships for a foreign power . . . would be definitely contrary to the policy of the Government."[71] And so it went. The State Department was willing to approve the export licenses in this case (and in others), but its officials believed that "subordinate officers in the Navy Department have repeatedly told the ship builders and the representatives of the other interested American companies not to enter into contracts with representatives of the U.S.S.R."[72] Navy officers also raised the issue of time and the Neutrality Act of 1935. If a ship was still under construction in the United States when the buyer and another nation went to war, the uncompleted ship would be impounded by the United States. If Russia went to war with Germany or Japan, it could lose its whole investment. The State Department confirmed this to the Soviet ambassador.[73]

The merry-go-round kept spinning through the fall of 1939. Roosevelt said he wanted the Navy to help the Soviet government. In 1938, however, the State Department said that the very large battleship that the Soviet government wanted to build with U.S. help was *too large*—it ran way over the limits set in the London Naval Agreement of 1936 and was endangering negotiations with the British. Admiral Leahy told the representatives of Carp and Amtorg that they could not deal with a shipbuilder unless they also allowed the Navy to review the design that architect William F. Gibbs (vice president of Gibbs and Cox) had drawn up for them. Waiting on the State Department and the Navy, though, had its costs: the export licenses had to be renewed annually, adding further to the delay. Even Joseph Stalin got involved. He could not understand why the wheels of government turned but nothing happened.

Nothing happened because Roosevelt would not make it happen. He wanted to show symbolic support for the Soviet government, but he was not eager for more—unlike later, once the USSR was at war with Germany. The runaround suited him. Everyone passed the buck. State Department officials told the Soviet representatives that the problem—if any—was one for the Navy to solve. Admiral Leahy said there were problems with the Espionage Act of 1917. Then, when the USSR's wishes for a large, heavily armed warship (indeed, a hybrid battleship–aircraft carrier designed especially for them by W. F. Gibbs himself)[74] were clear to him, Leahy sent the Russians back to the State Department. State said "wait." Then, when the State Department approved the deal in principle, industry balked, blaming lower-level Navy officers. Any further progress usually fell on the stake of the requirement to approve export licenses every year. One wonders why the Soviet government persevered. The only benefit it received in the whole affair was the establishment of "legitimate" import-export firms like Amtorg in the United States. The latter was later used, during World War II, as a cover for espionage.

The case of the Navy and the USSR shows Roosevelt as—to use the term applied by James M. Burns—the fox. If there were a way to help the Soviet government, then Roosevelt would do it. But the issue was not important enough for him then to intervene personally, as he could—and did—in other cases. Similarly, he supported naval rearmament because shipbuilding could be justified as a means of reducing unemployment. But he never went head-to-head with those members of Congress who held strong views about American neutrality. Ships could be justified as "required" by treaty. Personnel increases, on the other hand, were strictly limited, despite the problems that caused senior Navy leaders.[75]

Admiral Leahy described Roosevelt's style judiciously: the president "had little confidence in some of his executive departments, and therefore took detailed action with his own hands. . . . This permitted President Roosevelt to be completely familiar with the details of all of his written orders and other official communications."[76] But Leahy was a favorite of the president. He was comfortable with his chief (as his wartime service showed) and able to work *with* Roosevelt.

But doing so took some nerve, and much patience. For example, Jeffrey Dorwart has documented the president's use of the Office of Naval Intelligence for political purposes.[77] Roosevelt took a great risk, not just by chancing that his relationship with ONI might be revealed publicly, but also by exposing himself *and his office* to pressure from intelligence officers. Yet his circle of talented friends and contacts, and even his liberal image—one not generally favored by Navy officers—was some protection against such a challenge from within ONI.[78] In 1935, for example, the commander of the Special Service Squadron in the Caribbean sent a memo to the chief of naval operations expressing concern about the president's appointee as governor of the Virgin Islands. The memo was routed through ONI, and the latter argued that the president's appointee, who favored more economic and political opportunities for the black population, was setting a standard that might encourage demands for more opportunity—more freedom—by the black citizens of the continental United States. Admiral Standley, the chief of naval operations, ordered that both the memo and ONI's cover letter not be circulated further.[79] Whatever Admiral Standley's personal and professional views of this matter were, one thing was clear: the president's political choices and views on race relations were not to be attacked in formal memos or correspondence.

Despite his liberal ideas and image, however, Roosevelt had not integrated the Navy. But he had allowed Mrs. Roosevelt to pressure the service by writing directly to Secretary Swanson, asking why black sailors were not eligible for most ratings open to enlisted personnel. Swanson had answered her by explaining that the reason why black sailors were confined to positions as messmen was because any other policy would allow them to compete for positions as petty officers, where they would be "in charge of and have under them white men."[80] One can imagine Mrs. Roosevelt's response to *that*. The president could placate Swanson and senior naval officers by pointing to Mrs. Roosevelt's well-known and very public views and her independence. But Mrs. Roosevelt had sent the right message: the president would accept racial segregation in the Navy (even if his wife knew this to be an injustice), but he would make sure that the leaders of the service knew that he did not support it.

James M. Burns described this presidential style very well: "raising goals, creating momentum, inspiring a personal loyalty, getting the best out of people; . . . skillful timing . . . maintaining an extremely wide 'span of control' . . . often delving into specific, even tiny matters . . . maintaining his own private storehouse of intelligence . . . retiring behind the protection of rules, customs, conventions when they served his needs and evading them when they did not—and always . . . persuading, flattering, juggling, improvising, reshuffling, harmonizing, conciliating, manipulating."[81] American citizens and historians are now accustomed to this image of Franklin Roosevelt. It takes an outsider like John Keegan, in his own history of the Second World War, to remind us that Roosevelt's Machiavellian style was, for his contemporaries and his subordinates, simultaneously exciting, perplexing, and even sinister. Navy leaders, particularly the chiefs of naval operations, both enjoyed and resented the President's attention. What they wanted from him was permission to expand the Navy and then his strong support in Congress to obtain funds to pay for that expansion. What Roosevelt gave them was support, but with a catch: he would dictate the pace and the nature of that expansion.

Roosevelt as Strategist

Presidents must lead foreign policy or be led by foreign events. Presidents can either react to events, developing a strategy piecemeal, or they can develop a national strategy, gain support for it in Congress and the public, and then implement it. On the highest level, Franklin Roosevelt appears to have been a master strategist. In 1933, his primary goal was to hold the United States together and prevent a repeat of the fascist coups that had put parliamentary democracy at bay in much of Europe. His primary concern was for the survival of an open, relatively free, and productive society. The main threat to the survival of that society was internal—the lack of employment and of the prosperity that employment brought in its wake. The president was preoccupied with that immediate and terribly real threat.

Roosevelt could not, however, ignore the problems and obligations left him by his predecessors in the field of international affairs. Within the constraints of domestic politics, he moved quickly to improve relations with the nations of Central and South America (the Good Neighbor Policy was announced in April

1933). Then, as his next step, Roosevelt gained approval of a program to modernize and enlarge the Navy (the Naval Parity Act of March 1934), bringing it up to the standards authorized by the Washington Treaty. The president also reaffirmed the support of the government of the United States for the concept of naval arms limitation by welcoming the convening of the London Conference in December 1935. Though Japan and Italy refused to continue the naval force ratios that had been set in Washington in 1922, the government of the United States continued to exercise restraint in the production of warships—not appropriating funds, for example, for the construction of new battleships until the fiscal year 1938 (summer 1937).

The government of the United States also reacted deliberately and diplomatically when gunboat *Panay* was sunk by Japanese air attack on the Yangtze in December 1937. In 1938, the president asked for—and Congress granted—an increase in the size of the United States Fleet. The justification was to maintain the nation's "first line of defense." The goal was to isolate conflict in Europe and Asia—to keep it away from the Western Hemisphere. That same year, the Joint Planning Committee of the Joint Board of the Army and Navy began drawing up estimates of what force levels would be needed were the United States to find itself in a two-front war.

The rest of the story—the shift from neutrality to armed neutrality and thence to belligerence—has been told elsewhere in great detail.[82] Seen from our time, Roosevelt's overall strategy seems coherent. First he deals with domestic problems and issues festering in the Western Hemisphere. Then he pursues disarmament and negotiations, adhering to treaty limits. Once those policies have been discredited by other nations, he gradually begins a program of rearmament, though the emphasis remains on defense—first of the United States proper and then of the whole Western Hemisphere. As threats from two oceans mount, he improves relations with Britain and buys time with diplomacy, waiting for public opinion to "catch up" with his desire to confront an aggressive Germany and Japan. Once war begins, he forges and maintains an unlikely and uneasy (but victorious) alliance. It all looks very sensible, thoughtfully incremental. But of course it was not. As Burns notes, Roosevelt both avoided making strategic decisions himself and "refused to let his military chiefs commit themselves on the most compelling matters."[83] George Baer was just as blunt: "Fundamental executive decisions were needed [in summer 1940] to guide naval strategy. Roosevelt waited."[84] Baer's words are worth repeating: "Roosevelt waited." He did not have a grand strategy, either for dealing with the Great Depression or for tackling international issues.

But though the president may have been an opportunist in making strategy, he was not—as commander in chief—without a plan. Burns again: "there was another Chief Executive who *had* long been concerned with orderly executive management . . . who had created the Executive Office of the President and by transferring the Budget Bureau into it had immensely strengthened central presidential control."[85] This was the Roosevelt who could see the value of using National Industrial Recovery Act funds meant to reduce unemployment in 1933 for shipbuilding—for sustaining a key industry and for building the Navy's strength at the same time. This was also the Roosevelt who, with Carl Vinson, persuaded the Congress to give the Navy a blanket authorization in 1934 that eliminated the need for the Navy's leaders to return annually to Congress to request both authorizations *and* appropriations for ship construction. And this was the Roosevelt who had persuaded Congress to pass the Merchant Marine Act of 1936—surely one of the most essential steps in preparing the nation for a two-ocean war.

The president was not an ad hoc manager of the nation's military institutions. As Burns argued in his careful study of Roosevelt, the president guarded his power, so that he remained "Chief Executive in fact as well as in title."[86] Roosevelt did so by intervening, initiating, and directing in a calculated—not random—way. His symbolic support for the Navy is well documented. He *did* like the Navy more than the Army, and he showed it. Yet he did not want to be seen as a "Navy man," especially by the leaders of that service. They had to understand that he was not in their pockets. They also had to grasp that he did not need to bargain with them for their support. Roosevelt needed to guard his constitutional authority, and he did.

Yet Robert Levine was quite right to title his study of the Roosevelt administration's fundamental naval policy *The Politics of American Naval Rearmament*. The stress should be on the word "politics." Roosevelt was a "political" planner, not a "strategic" one. As Burns put it, Roosevelt "had long been a planner. . . . But planning, to Roosevelt, was a sharply limited exercise. It was segmental."[87] That is, it was political, in the sense that political objectives in a pluralistic society must be "segmental" because pluralistic societies tend to lack overarching *strategic objectives*. Objectives are worked out as people go along, through negotiation. Strategic objectives reached through pluralistic bargaining tend to be both grand ("making the world safe for democracy") and ill defined.

So Roosevelt could build up the fleet by appealing to vague but generally accepted national ideals and, simultaneously, by bargaining with particular interests (who wanted jobs or production contracts). Levine's work makes that very clear. What should also be clear is that this approach produced what in retrospect looks like a strategy, even though there was no grand conceptual strategy in the president's head. This worked well in peacetime, but it had dire consequences in wartime and particularly after the war, as Burns has pointed out.[88]

It also placed a great strain on the Navy's uniformed leaders. In 1933, their primary concern was to build the Navy to "treaty" strength, and the likely enemy was Japan. After 1936, with the naval arms limitation "system" in ruins, their concern was to lay the foundation for steady growth. After Munich, they began planning for a possible two-ocean war. After the fall of France in 1940, all bets were off. Congress gushed a veritable geyser of money, and the Navy mushroomed in size. Before the French army was defeated, the U.S. Navy had under construction 52 warships and 62 auxiliaries. By February 1941, there were 368 warships and 338 auxiliaries on the building ways.[89]

Ship Design: Roosevelt's Hobby

As my friend Wayne Hughes has observed, President Roosevelt frequently "dabbled" in his hobby of ship design. Sometimes he was remarkably perceptive. Consider the development and production of destroyer escorts and escort aircraft carriers once war threatened. The president actively supported the development of both types of ship. In the summer of 1940, for example, Roosevelt reviewed schemes for a fast but small (only 1,050 tons) destroyer, and he ordered the Navy to purchase four of them, "even though they clearly had little to do with Navy requirements."[90] As Norman Friedman discovered, these small ships (too small for effective antisubmarine work) were not built. Instead, the order placed by the Navy's Bureau of Ships was "changed to four 1,175-ton units of BuShips design, which were the forerunners of the [destroyer escort]."[91]

Roosevelt's influence was even stronger in the case of escort carriers. The Navy had long considered the conversion of large liners and other merchant ships to aircraft carriers in the event of war. The Navy's leaders had also debated at length the value of so-called flying-deck cruisers, hybrids with both guns and aircraft. Rear Admiral William A. Moffett, the first chief of the Bureau of Aeronautics, had pressed for the hybrid cruiser-carrier in 1931, and the General Board spent a great deal of time in the 1930s considering the possibility of devoting cruiser tonnage to the type.[92] The board rejected the idea for a number of reasons. Admiral Joseph M. Reeves, commander in chief of the United States Fleet, summed up the case against the flying-deck cruiser in a memo to the board dated October 8, 1934: "Each study shows it to be a hybrid type entirely unsuitable as a cruiser or as a carrier."[93] But the conversion of liners—attractive for the role of emergency carriers because of their large size—was both expensive and time consuming, and so the problem of emergency carriers for wartime use did not go away.

In October 1940, when President Roosevelt proposed to the chief of naval operations that the Navy convert a standard merchant ship design to a small aircraft carrier that could accompany convoys, the Navy's leaders faced a dilemma. Rear Admiral William Halsey, then commanding the carriers of the fleet's Battle Force, also wanted auxiliary carriers.[94] But how large should they be? Halsey, speaking for the Navy's aviators, recommended a flight deck 600 feet long—too long for standard merchant ship designs then building. A converted merchant ship could be produced relatively quickly, while the converted liner could not, but the Navy's aviators had doubts about the safety and effectiveness of the smaller type. Which aircraft could fly from the converted merchant ship hulls? And would each smaller carrier hold enough aircraft to make the conversion worthwhile? Most importantly, would the construction or conversion of such smaller, less-effective carriers deflect the regular carrier construction program? These were not minor questions.

To answer them, the chief of naval operations, Admiral Harold R. Stark, "held a series of conferences on merchant-ship conversions between 31 December 1940 and 23 January 1941."[95] The result was a decision to convert two standard (C-3) diesel-powered ships then being built. The president, following the course of the Navy's deliberations, pressed for speed. The Navy resisted. As Friedman put it, "the naval leadership wanted something close to a full carrier. Roosevelt knew he had to settle for less."[96] Roosevelt got what he wanted.

These cases were typical. The president *acted*, often on his own instincts and with the advice of personal acquaintances such as Francis Gibbs, the ship designer and head of the firm of Gibbs and

Cox, and the Navy's uniformed leaders *reacted*, usually negatively. The reason was simple: the Navy's uniformed leaders feared that "austere designs" built for war service *only* would in fact be forced on them after the war by a stingy Congress and a chief executive interested more in demobilization than in the modernization of a fleet worn down by the high tempo of war operations. The Navy had suffered through that once before. In 1940, it was still using 1,200-ton destroyers and even some 500-ton "eagle boats" (and a few wooden subchasers) built for the emergency antisubmarine campaign of World War I, and it did not want to be saddled with similar ships after the next war.[97]

But the president was commander in chief. Moreover, he had an interest in ship designs and enough knowledge of warships to be dangerous (from the perspective of his senior naval leaders). As Robert Levine noted in his *The Politics of American Naval Rearmament,* Roosevelt had extraordinary influence, before the war, in the Navy's Bureau of Construction and Repair (later merged, in 1940, with the Bureau of Engineering to form the Bureau of Ships) and Bureau of Navigation—that is, in the organizations responsible for ship design and personnel.[98] As the international situation grew more threatening, Roosevelt intervened more often. In 1939, he decided that carrier number 8, *Hornet,* would basically duplicate the already operational *Yorktown* and *Enterprise,* and he also pushed up the contract award date for the first of the *Iowa*-class battleships.[99] Later, he forced the Navy to convert light cruisers to light carriers. Roosevelt felt not the slightest hesitation in involving himself in matters of ship design. The president used Francis Gibbs and others as sounding boards for his own ideas. Roosevelt would not let his admirals retain the initiative in the field of ship design.

The real danger inherent in the president's "hobby" was that, in indulging him, Navy leaders ran the risk that Roosevelt would—through reckless overconfidence—make a serious error, especially in his use of the Navy as a strategic tool—an instrument of American policy. In this area, as in the field of naval architecture, he was confident in his own judgment. Once he became convinced that war was imminent, for example, he acted as commander in chief to place the Navy on a war footing, with the focus on a conflict in the Atlantic. His actions in the critical year leading up to Pearl Harbor have been described and analyzed well by historians such as Waldo Heinrichs.[100] One such deserves mention here: the decision to move the fleet to Hawaii. Admiral James O. Richardson, then commander in chief of the United States Fleet, was outraged by the order. His protests to Roosevelt were so strong that the president relieved him. Richardson's complaints were three: (1) that the fleet could not be supported by Pearl Harbor's repair and fuel facilities, (2) that the harbor was not deep and large enough for great numbers of heavy ships, and (3) that the move would not really deter Japan from further military action. The question of who was correct is not the issue here, though some evidence suggests Roosevelt was right.[101] The point is that the president had to have great self-confidence in order to reject the protests of so professional an officer. Roosevelt's successes in the *details* of naval administration gave him—as Admiral Leahy knew—the ability to make larger decisions with confidence.

Conclusion

Roosevelt, in short, could have the best of both worlds. He could, in the 1930s, indulge his personal interests in ship design and satisfy his political desire to reduce unemployment. He could play with the Navy as though it were a wonderful, magnificent toy while at the same time holding it on a tight fiscal leash. He could appoint men he trusted, like Leahy, to positions of leadership within the Navy without ever losing his authority and stature as commander in chief. He could—and did—improve the Navy's morale and material strength without at the same time provoking a backlash from the isolationists in Congress. In some sense, his lack of a grand strategic vision was an asset. He must always have had in mind Woodrow Wilson's failure because he avoided Wilson's mistakes.

When Roosevelt took the oath of office, he assumed command of a navy that needed funds, strategic guidance, and encouragement. He knew that, and he provided all three. In 1930, the Navy had 12 first-line battleships (only 3 of which mounted 16-inch guns), 5 new heavy cruisers, 10 older light cruisers, 2 modern carriers, 255 old destroyers, and 93 submarines, most of them older types. By 1940, there were still 12 first-line battleships (but 2 new ones were soon to be commissioned and another 4 were under construction), 18 heavy cruisers of the "treaty" type, 17 light cruisers (7 of them new), 6 carriers (a seventh would be completed in 1941), 74 new destroyers, and 32 new submarines.[102] The new destroyers and submarines were in addition to the many older, obsolescent types. By 1940, the Navy possessed the "balanced fleet" that the Navy's General Board had pressed for over the previous two decades: a mix of battleships, carriers, cruisers, destroyers, and submarines that could take on the tasks assigned them by the Orange Plan in a trans-Pacific campaign.

In 1933, Roosevelt had found himself in command of a fleet that wasn't really a fleet. He allowed that fleet to expand and to modernize in the 1930s—and to operate. It was not enough just to have the fleet increase in size. It had to exercise; it had to be maintained; older but essential units, such as carriers *Lexington* and *Saratoga*, had to be modernized; new technologies—such as improved fire control devices—had to be developed and applied to existing ships. All this was done. In 1935, for example, Roosevelt and Vinson together persuaded the Congress to raise the statutory ceiling on ship repairs that had been in place (in Title 5, U.S.C.) since 1916.[103] This gave the CNO and the chiefs of the Bureau of Steam Engineering and the Bureau of Construction and Repair much greater freedom to schedule and complete overhauls and modifications. Naval technology changed rapidly in the 1930s, and the modification in the law allowed the Navy to invest its scarce funds in upgrades in a more intelligent and less time-consuming way.

If there was anything the commander in chief did not provide, it was the requirement to develop a navy for a two-ocean war. That came late, with the Naval Expansion Act of 1940, passed by the Congress in June 1940 after the fall of France. The Navy's singular focus on the Pacific was an obstacle to global war planning by 1940, but the president dared not force its revision until isolationist legislators were persuaded by events that the threat on the Atlantic side was even more grave than that from the Pacific theater.

Once the political support for massive arms production coalesced, however, the industrial base existed to turn political will into a huge fleet. The shipbuilding portion of that industrial base had been built up gradually because of the passage of the Naval Parity (or Vinson-Trammell) Act of 1934 and the Merchant Marine Act of 1936. Also in 1936, the secretaries of War and the Navy approved an industrial mobilization plan that specified in detail the emergency powers (such as eminent domain and compulsory orders to industry) that the president would have to have in wartime. That same year, Congress gave the president the power to purchase or confiscate privately owned merchant ships in the event of any declared national emergency. Three years later, Roosevelt, acting on his own authority, placed under his direct control the offices of the Army chief of staff and the chief of naval operations, the Army-Navy Munitions Board, the Aeronautical Board, and the Joint Economy Board(where service representatives could discuss mobilization issues with the staffs of the secretaries of treasury and commerce). Congress soon thereafter passed the Reorganization Act of 1939, which created the Executive Office of the President and also gave Roosevelt the authority to set up agencies that he judged essential to the nation's defense.[104] These were the legal steps upon which mobilization was built.

But preparing for war was a hit-and-miss business. For example, the Navy's Bureau of Ordnance (BuOrd) was faced with the consequences of a loss of much essential expertise because warship construction simply tailed off after the Washington Treaty was signed in 1922. The steel industry lost the capacity to produce *modern* armor, and the machine-tool industry, essential to the production of guns and ammunition, was kept alive economically during the first few years of the Great Depression only by foreign orders.[105] BuOrd officers and civilians responded to these emergencies by gathering documents and data from manufacturers, keeping track of skilled artisans, and organizing a machine-tool catalogue that "listed all applicable types of machine tools and plant equipment by function, then by source of manufacture and supply." IBM "machine accounting" kept track of critical machine tools in government and private hands, and projections of what would be needed for mobilization were accurate enough so that "ordnance establishments and a few major contractors were relatively well tooled at the time of the Japanese attack."[106] This sort of thing is what a good bureaucracy is supposed to do, and, in the Navy's case, it was done often enough, though the president neither directed it nor knew of it. But his actions did facilitate it, and that is what mattered.

Roosevelt also kept the Navy alive as a separate institution. Through the 1930s, there was an elaborate back-and-forth between the Congress and the executive branch over the proper organization of the nation's defense. Starting in June 1933, Representative Vinson introduced draft legislation to reorganize first the Navy and then both the War and Navy Departments. He had several goals. The first was to streamline and make more efficient the management of the departments by centralizing authority within them. For example, Vinson's 1933 proposal aimed to consolidate control over the Navy's bureaus under a director of naval materiel, an admiral who would have served alongside the chief of naval operations and be directly subordinate to the secretary of the Navy.[107] Later proposals, by Vinson and by others in Congress, raised an issue that had come up often since World War I: the organizational status of military aviation. That particular issue had been a contentious one in 1925, when Army Brigadier General William Mitchell had called for the creation of a separate military department for aviation. After two special boards had considered the issue, Congress chose not to combine the aviation components of the Army and Navy into a separate military department. But in the 1930s, with the military role of aviation growing, pressure grew to create a separate organization for military aviation *within* a department of defense. Vinson and others doubted the ability of the separate War and Navy Departments to produce the materiel and the forces necessary for an adequate national defense in what was becoming an increasingly technological era.

The issue was a real one, and it is still with us. It pits against one another two views about how military organizations ought to be structured. The first view holds that "control" is the key factor, and that centralized authority is the key to control. The second view is based upon a fear of overcentralization and maintains that centralized authority actually inhibits innovation and the ability of an organization (especially a military one) to learn from its mistakes. Though he supported the Navy (the Vinson-Trammell Act is just one of his contributions to naval expansion), Congressman Vinson was also critical of the way the Navy Department was organized and administered. He was also accustomed to being listened to. In December 1931, for example, Rear Admiral William Moffett, then chief of the Bureau of Aeronautics, had penned these words to the Georgia representative: "Upon my return from the flight of the *Akron* over your district, . . . the thought occurred to me, as I looked over the country and the cities, that the people were all your friends and how fortunate they are to have you represent them in Congress."[108] Clearly, Vinson was both knowledgeable and influential. His ideas were neither dismissed out of hand nor ignored within the Navy Department. But ultimately it was Roosevelt who had to protect the Navy from reorganization proposals that Navy leaders thought unwise. Their opposition to the centralized management of defense—a position they maintained through the 1950s—was one that Roosevelt tacitly accepted.

It is also important to note here that the "balanced" fleet constructed during the 1930s did not simply fall into place. It was *made*—through exercises, through training, and after experiments in war games and fleet problems. Furthermore, what ships and aircraft the Navy possessed affected what it could do, which further influenced what ships and aircraft it wanted and the tactics it developed for combat. An example is the carrier task force. As Henry Dater noted as long ago as 1950, "What the Navy lacked more than anything else [in the years before World War II] was sufficient numbers of carriers to form an effective task force. . . . the concentration of power in a true carrier task force remained to be developed."[109] The danger of concentrating carriers together was clear: they could all be wiped out in one surprise attack, like the Japanese navy's carriers at the Battle of Midway in June 1942. However, combining carrier air groups maximized the power of their attack aircraft, so there was a trade-off between the need to maximize attack strength and the need to disperse carriers so that they would survive an initial attack. This trade-off needed to be analyzed, but could not be explored in practice because there were not enough carriers (only six by 1940) to set up two opposing task forces and pit them against one another in mock battle. Even the Japanese did not exercise with large (four and six) carrier task forces until 1941, when two new carriers brought their total strength to eight. And even then they had little time to really experiment.

It is easy to forget that it takes time to mold an effective combat force. And, once molded, that force may have to be remolded because of changes in technology and discoveries made during tactical exercises. In the 1930s, technology advanced in several critical areas. Fire control improved drastically, for example, and the consequences were visible in the ships themselves. Battleships such as *Nevada* and *Arizona* emerged from modernization during the Hoover administration with tall tripod masts that housed their main (14-inch guns) target-spotting equipment and secondary (5-inch guns) fire control directors. *Idaho* and her two sisters, by contrast, did not have tall masts to house spotting equipment for their 14-inch guns when they rejoined the fleet in 1933. Instead, long-range fire was to be directed by the battleships' own spotting aircraft, and the ships' superstructures were crowned by a dual-purpose secondary director (indicating the importance of warding off aircraft attack). The same change in technology produced a similar alteration of appearance as the newer heavy cruisers (such as *Astoria*) joined the fleet alongside earlier types such as *Houston,* which had tall foremasts for spotting gunfire.

Change was even more rapid in aircraft. Planes got heavier, flew faster, were armored, increased their combat ranges, and carried significantly more ordnance. This was the result of a deliberate policy developed within, and then implemented by, the Navy's Bureau of Aeronautics.[110] Aeronautics promoted the development of more powerful engines, and the more powerful engines made possible higher wing loadings (85 percent of takeoff weight divided by wing area), which in turn meant greater speeds for climbing, cruising, and diving. The wing loading (pounds per square foot) of the Grumman F3F-1 biplane fighter of 1935 was 13.53. That of the monoplane F4F-4 of 1941 was 26.07. The Curtiss SBC-4 biplane scout bomber, which first flew in 1934, had a loaded weight of 7,632 lbs. and carried a 1,000 lb. bomb. The Douglas SBD-5, the first model of which took to the air in the summer of 1935, had a loaded weight of 10,403 lbs. and carried 1,600 lbs. of ordnance. The contracts for the procurement of these two aircraft were signed just over two years apart—in June 1932 and November 1934, respectively. The growth in size and performance is impressive, and it continued: the next scout dive bomber was the Curtiss SB2C, the contract for which was signed in May 1939. The SB2C had a loaded weight of 14,415 lbs. (in the SB2C-5 model) and an ordnance load of 3,000 lbs.[111] This rapid growth in size and performance meant that carriers had to operate planes that were heavier and larger than those flying or even planned at the time the carriers were designed. It also meant that naval architects had to design surface warships such as cruisers and battleships to withstand the heavier bombs and more powerful torpedoes that these new aircraft could carry.

The problems produced by this rapid technological change were many. No matter how perceptive and active President Roosevelt was, he could not solve them. He could—and did— persuade the Congress to authorize ship construction and aircraft procurement and appropriate the funds to purchase the ships and planes. He could appoint leaders he thought best for the Navy and then use his constitutional power to influence their decisions about ship design, personnel levels, the selection process for officers, and naval force levels. But he could not become involved in the technical trade-off process that went on constantly within the Navy, nor could he supervise the development of naval tactics, nor could he predict the path of technological change. These matters had to be left to the professionals. They were the ones who had both the expertise and the resources to develop electronic warfare (especially code breaking, but also radar and sonar), amphibious operations, and the staff expertise necessary for the planning and execution of ocean-spanning campaigns.

Where Roosevelt made his greatest contribution was as chief executive, particularly in providing the Navy with funds, with new ship authorizations, with better pay, and with higher morale. He also understood that the United States needed friends instead of enemies in its strategic "back yard," and that the Navy was a tool to implement the diplomacy that he favored. Roosevelt also provided the Navy with leadership. Secretary Swanson, portrayed often as a figure without much influence, has perhaps been underrated. Robert Levine seems to think so, and I think Levine is correct. Indeed, it would have been difficult for any Navy secretary to exercise influence with Roosevelt in the White House, Carl

Vinson as head of the Naval Affairs Committee in the House of Representatives, and James Byrnes as chairman of the naval sub-committee of the Senate Appropriations Committee.

Chiefs of Naval Operations William D. Leahy (1937-1939) and Harold Stark (1939-1942) were talented officers and were able to work well with the persuasive, intrusive, often frustrating commander in chief. As the world situation worsened, they responded with expanded strategic views. Stark basically drafted American strategy in the fall of 1940, partly to force the president to make some hard choices, and Roosevelt brought Leahy back from retirement to serve as his chief of staff during the war. And of course Roosevelt's appointment of Admiral Ernest J. King as commander in chief of the United States Fleet was inspired.

So the president did have an impact—a critical one. Another way of demonstrating the point is by asking what would have happened if Roosevelt had not been president—would the Navy have developed the key factors that brought it victory in the Atlantic and Pacific? The question can be put another way: what if Herbert Hoover had served two terms and then had been followed by another Republican? In 1932 and early 1933, would the Navy have recovered from the doldrums it was in when the chief of naval operations, Admiral Pratt, was at his wits' end trying to maintain the Navy as a force sufficient to deter Japanese advances in the Pacific? A second Hoover administration would have been very hard on the Navy—not because President Hoover wished to eliminate the Navy, but because he had doubts about the international policy that the Navy was intended to help implement. Admiral Pratt had argued in vain for permission to ask Congress for a modern navy capable of enforcing the Washington Treaty of 1922. Hoover had doubts about the value of the Navy (or any military force) as a tool for enforcing the agreements.

In one sense, Hoover was correct. If Japan wished to abandon the Washington Treaty and what it stood for, an American "treaty" navy would not stop her. But what President Hoover ignored was the need to modernize and enlarge the Navy in order to deter Japan from assaulting the United States. So long as the United States possessed the Philippines, American military power could not be ignored by Japan. So long as American military power gave Japanese leaders pause, the Pacific remained relatively peaceful. The Washington Conference of 1921-1922 had created a delicate balance between the United States and Japan in the Pacific. The Navy was an essential weight on the American side of that balance. It had to be maintained in sufficient strength in the Pacific in order to sustain the balance. Roosevelt understood this better than Hoover. Or perhaps it is better to say he accepted it while Hoover did not wish to. What matters is that Roosevelt's efforts to bring the Navy to "treaty strength" laid the foundations—political, military, and industrial—for the expansions after 1938 and 1940. A second Hoover administration would probably have done the reverse, retarding the expansion required once Japan had decided to abandon the "treaty system."

NOTES

1. Professor Wayne Hughes, letter to author, Dec. 26, 1996.
2. Ibid. Prof. Hughes believes that Roosevelt's "grand instinct" was evident when he took the oath of office in 1933. I wonder. On April 10, 1933, the secretary of the Navy sent a memo to "All Bureaus and Offices, Navy Dept." The subject of that memo was "Reduction in Expenditures for Fiscal Year 1934," and the news was bad, indeed. The memo is in file "Organization of the Navy Department," General Board Study, Record Group (RG) 80, no. 446, Naval Historical Center. The memo is SONYD-C-Kr-4/8, (SC) L1-1 (1934). See also Craig L. Symonds, "William Veazie Pratt," in *The Chiefs of Naval Operations,* ed. R. W. Love, Jr. (Annapolis: Naval Institute Press, 1980), esp. 84.
3. James M. Burns, *Roosevelt: The Soldier of Freedom* (New York: Harcourt Brace Jovanovich, 1970), 352.
4. John Prados, *Combined Fleet Decoded* (New York: Random House, 1995), Chaps. 2-5. See also J. N. Wenger, "Military Study: Communication Intelligence Research Activities," June 30, 1937, SRH 151, RG 457, National Archives.

5. Wenger, "Military Study: Communication Intelligence Research Activities," 9.

6. For Problem XV, see *CINCUS Report*, June 1, 1934, "Exercise N," p. 54, Records of the Office of the Chief of Naval Operations, RG 38, National Archives. For Problem XVI, see *CINCUS Report*, Sept. 15, 1935, "Critique of Fleet Problem 16 Held at San Diego, California 15 June 1935," Remarks of Vice Admiral H. V. Butler, 1, Records of the Office of the Chief of Naval Operations, RG 38. For Problem XX, see "Fleet Problem XX, Comments and Recommendations," from Commanding Officer *USS Ranger* to CINCUS, Mar. 31, 1939 (CV4/A16-3/FPXX), roll 26, U.S. Navy Fleet Problems, RG 38, National Archives.

7. C-in-C, U.S. Fleet, memo to Chief of Naval Operations, "Absence of Press Correspondents and Photographers in U.S. Fleet during Fleet Problem XVII," May 9, 1936, file no. (5C)A16-3(5-XVII), RG 38, National Archives.

8. W. J. Holmes, *Double-Edged Secrets: U.S. Naval Intelligence Operations in the Pacific During World War II* (Annapolis: Naval Institute Press, 1979).

9. Commander Aircraft, Battle Force, to CINC U.S. Fleet, "Comments and Recommendations—Fleet Problem XVIII," June 4, 1937, 7, microfilm roll 23, U.S. Navy Fleet Problems, RG 38, National Archives.

10. Ibid., 4.

11. Thomas Wildenberg, *Gray Steel and Black Oil* (Annapolis: Naval Institute Press, 1996), 128-131, 181.

12. F. C. Lane, *Ships for Victory: A History of Shipbuilding under the U.S. Maritime Commission in World War II* (Baltimore: Johns Hopkins Press, 1951).

13. Clark Reynolds, *The Fast Carriers: The Forging of an Air Navy* (New York: McGraw-Hill, 1968; reprint, Annapolis: Naval Institute Press, 1992), 86 (page citations are to the reprint edition).

14. Reynolds, *Fast Carriers*, 54-55.

15. Memo from Rear Admiral Frederick Sherman to Pacific Fleet commander Admiral Chester Nimitz, September 5, 1943, in Reynolds, *Fast Carriers*, 46.

16. Eliot Cohen and John Gooch, *Military Misfortunes: The Anatomy of Failure in War* (New York: Macmillan, 1990), 74; citing "Status of Available Surface Forces, North Atlantic Naval Coastal Frontier," Dec. 22, 1941, *Eastern Sea Frontier War Diary*, December 1941, 30, U.S. Navy Operational Archives, Naval Historical Center.

17. Thomas C. Hone, "The Effectiveness of the 'Washington Treaty' Navy," *Naval War College Review*, 32, no. 6 (Nov.-Dec. 1979), 50.

18. Cohen and Gooch, *Military Misfortunes*, 87-88.

19. "Exercise Plan No. 3-19A," Mar. 28, 1938 (A4-3/11-Fd/FF2-3), Fleet Problem XIX, microfilm roll 23, U.S. Navy Fleet Problems, RG 38, National Archives.

20. For a firsthand account of this problem, see Edward L. Beach, "Culpable Negligence," in *Eyewitness to World War II*, ed. Stephen W. Sears (Boston: Houghton Mifflin, 1991), 65-86.

21. Commander in Chief, U.S. Fleet, memo to Chief of Naval Operations, "Submarine Torpedo Attack on Fleet—Exercise No. 77, Week 4-8 April, Fleet Problem XIX, report of," (A16-3/FPXIX/0552), Apr. 27, 1938, "Inclosure B," p. 7, microfilm roll 23, U.S. Navy Fleet Problems, RG 38, National Archives.

22. Clay Blair, Jr., *Silent Victory: The U.S. Submarine War Against Japan* (Philadelphia: Lippincott, 1975).

23. For sonar development, see Norman Friedman, *U.S. Submarines through 1945* (Annapolis: Naval Institute Press, 1995), 197-98. For radar, see David K. Allison, *New Eye for the Navy: The Origins of Radar at the Naval Research Laboratory* (Washington, D.C.: GPO, 1981). The pulse and air defense radars are mentioned by the late Admiral H. G. Bowen in *Ships, Machinery and Mossbacks* (Princeton: Princeton Univ. Press, 1954), 142-43.

24. *Hearings of the General Board of the Navy*, "Characteristics of Capital Ships," September 13, 1937, no. 246, p. 11. These records were in the Navy's Operational Archives. They are now in the National Archives.

25. See Charles D. Allen, "Forecasting Future Forces," *United States Naval Institute Proceedings* (Nov. 1982), vol. 108.

26. Norman Friedman, *U.S. Naval Weapons* (London: Conway Maritime Press, 1983).

27. See Buford Rowland and William Boyd, *U.S. Navy Bureau of Ordnance in World War II* (Washington: GPO, 1953).

28. Harvey Sapolsky, *Science and the Navy: The History of the Office of Naval Research* (Princeton: Princeton Univ. Press, 1990), 11-18.

29. See R. D. Heinl, *Soldiers of the Sea: The United States Marine Corps, 1775-1962* (Annapolis: U.S. Naval Institute, 1962), and A. R. Millett, *Semper Fidelis: The History of the United States Marine Corps* (New York: Macmillan, 1980).

30. Commander in Chief, U.S. Fleet, memo to the Chief of Naval Operations, Feb. 1, 1934, "Utilization of Fleet Marine Force in Fleet Problem XV," in *CINCUS Report,* Fleet Problem XV.

31. *Hearings of the General Board of the Navy,* "Procurement of Airplanes for Fleet Marine Force," Sept. 22, 1938, no. 128, 40.

32. Jeter A. Isely and Philip A. Crowl, *The U.S. Marines and Amphibious War: Its Theory, and Its Practice in the Pacific* (Princeton: Princeton Univ. Press, 1951).

33. Thomas C. Hone, "Naval Reconstitution, Surge, and Mobilization," *Naval War College Review* 47, no. 3 (June 1994), 72. See also, Lane, *Ships for Victory,* p. 23.

34. Lane, *Ships for Victory,* 5-8.

35. J. B. Hattendorf, B. M. Simpson III, and J. R. Wadleigh, *Sailors and Scholars: The Centennial History of the U.S. Naval War College* (Newport, R. I.: Naval War College Press, 1984), 141.

36. Hattendorf, Simpson, and Wadleigh, *Sailors and Scholars,* 158.

37. Edward S. Miller, *War Plan Orange: The U.S. Strategy to Defeat Japan* (Annapolis: Naval Institute Press, 1991), 184.
38. Ibid., 220-22.
39. Secretary of the Navy, memo to All Bureaus and Offices, Navy Dept., subject: "Reduction in Expenditures for Fiscal Year 1934," April 10, 1933, SONYD-C-Kr-4/8, (SC) L1-1 (1934), in "Organization of the Navy Department," General Board Studies No. 446, Jan. 24, 1934, RG 80, Naval Historical Center microfilm.
40. Thomas C. Hone, "Spending Patterns of the United States Navy, 1921-1941," *Armed Forces and Society* 8, no. 3 (spring 1982), 447, table 1.
41. Gerald E. Wheeler, "Charles Francis Adams," in *American Secretaries of the Navy* 2, ed. Paolo E. Coletta (Annapolis: Naval Institute Press, 1980), 645.
42. Robert H. Levine, *The Politics of American Naval Rearmament, 1930-1938* (New York: Garland Publishing, 1988), 377.
43. Wheeler, "Charles Francis Adams," 640.
44. Levine, *Politics of American Naval Rearmament*, 376.
45. Samuel Eliot Morison, *History of U.S. Naval Operations in World War II*, 3 (Boston: Little, Brown, 1959), 31, n. 20.
46. Allison Saville, "Claude Augustus Swanson," in *American Secretaries of the Navy*, ed. Coletta, 662.
47. Between 1933 and 1939, the number of battleships in commission stayed constant. The carriers *Yorktown* and *Enterprise* were added, which increased the carrier total from 3 to 5. Seven heavy cruisers of the *New Orleans* type were added to the 10 in service in 1933. Seven light cruisers of the *Brooklyn* class were added to the 10 *Omaha* class light cruisers in service in 1933. Sixty-one new destroyers and destroyer leaders joined the fleet between 1933 and 1939, and 28 new submarines. The question is how to count the older destroyers and submarines. On June 30, 1934, the Bureau of Construction and Repair listed 4 not overage destroyers and 99 overage destroyers, plus 42 not overage submarines and 13 overage. For September 30, 1939, the figures provided by the bureau were 63 not overage destroyers and 75 overage, plus 28 not overage submarines and 32 overage. During that period, then, the number of *total* destroyers increased from 103 to 138, but the number of *not overage* destroyers increased from 4 to 63. The total number of submarines stayed about the same—55 in 1934 and 60 in 1939—but the number of not overage submarines *declined* from 41 to 27. See two memos dated 1934 and 1939 from Bureau of Construction and Repair to General Board "Summary of Vessels of the United States Navy," A9-11-(4)(RP), boxes 54 and 55, General Board, subject file 420, RG 80, National Archives.
48. Hone, "Spending Patterns," 443-62.
49. Thomas Wildenberg, "Preparing for War: Admiral William H. Standley and the Struggle to Build Auxiliaries for the Navy," copy of paper in author's possession.
50. Symonds, "William Veazie Pratt," p. 84.
51. Wheeler, "Charles Francis Adams," 636-37.

52. John C. Walter, "William Harrison Standley," in *The Chiefs of Naval Operations*, ed. Love, 92.
53. Ibid.
54. Ibid.
55. Ibid.
56. FDR, letter to secretary of the Navy, Mar. 2, 1934, in "Organization of the Navy Department," General Board Study no. 446, RG 80, Naval Historical Center microfilm.
57. Chief of the Bureau of Navigation, memo to General Board, "Bill for the Reorganization of the Navy Department and for Amalgamation of certain Corps with the line as proposed by Congressman Vinson," Jan. 10, 1934, Nav-HH, EN/a3-1(4), 4; "Organization of the Navy Department," General Board Study No. 446, RG 80, Naval Historical Center microfilm.
58. CNO, memo to All Bureaus and Offices, "Ship Development Board," Sept. 5, 1934, Op-23-RSM, QB(94)/A3-1 (340905), para. 5; in "Organization of the Navy Department," RG 80, Naval Historical Center microfilm.
59. CNO, memo to Bureau Chiefs, "New Construction; Coordination of work of Bureaus in connection with, By Chief of Naval Operations," Sept. 24, 1934, Op-23-RSM, FS/L8-3(340921), paras 2 and 3, "Organization of the Navy Department," RG 80, Naval Historical Center microfilm.
60. Admiral W. S. Pye, "The Organization of the Navy Department," lecture to the Army Industrial College Class of 1936-37, in "Organization of the Navy Department," RG 80, Naval Historical Center microfilm.
61. Miller, *War Plan Orange,* 180-82; quotation at 180.
62. Walter, "William Harrison Standley," 97.
63. William D. Leahy, *I Was There* (New York: McGraw-Hill, 1950), 3.
64. Ibid., 8.
65. Department of State, *Foreign Relations of the United States (FRUS), The Soviet Union, 1933-1939* (Washington, D.C.: GPO, 1952), 457-59.
66. Ibid., 461.
67. Norman Friedman, *U.S. Destroyers: An Illustrated Design History* (Annapolis: Naval Institute Press, 1982), 88.
68. *FRUS,* 465.
69. Ibid., 468.
70. Ibid., 469-70.
71. Ibid., 478-79.
72. Ibid., 489. John Major, "William Daniel Leahy," in *The Chiefs of Naval Operations,* ed. Love. 108, says Leahy opposed the deal with the Soviet Union "from start to finish . . . allowing his subordinates . . . to run the project into the sand."
73. *FRUS, Soviet Union,* 490.
74. For a description of the ship, see *Hearings Before the General Board of the Navy, 1939* 1, "Battleship 'X,'" Dec. 5, 1939, Naval Historical Center microfilm.
75. Saville, "Claude Augustus Swanson," 662.

76. Leahy, *I Was There*, 5.

77. Jeffrey M. Dorwart, *Conflict of Duty: The U.S. Navy's Intelligence Dilemma, 1919-1945* (Annapolis: Naval Institute Press, 1983).

78. See Brian R. Sullivan, "'A Highly Commendable Action': William J. Donovan's Intelligence Mission for Mussolini and Roosevelt, December 1935-February 1936," *Intelligence and National Security* 6, no. 2 (Apr. 1991), 334-66.

79. Commander, U.S. Special Service Squadron, memo to Chief of Naval Operations, "Conditions in Virgin Islands," August 17, 1935 (Op-16-B-3, A8-2/EG 56 with A8-2/EG 56 [1208]), Office of the Secretary of the Navy, Confidential Correspondence file, 1927-1939, box 216, RG 80, National Archives.

80. Thomas B. Buell, *The Quiet Warrior* (Annapolis: Naval Institute Press, 1987), 68.

81. Burns, *Roosevelt: The Soldier of Freedom*, 349-50.

82. See George Baer, *One Hundred Years of Seapower* (Stanford: Stanford Univ. Press, 1994); John Major, "The Navy Plans for War," in *In Peace and War*, ed. Kenneth Hagan (Westport, Conn: Greenwood Press, 1984), 237-62; W. L. Langer and S. E. Gleason, *The Undeclared War, 1940-1941* (Gloucester, Mass: Peter Smith, 1968); and Waldo Heinrichs, *Threshold of War: Franklin D. Roosevelt and American Entry into World War II* (Oxford: Oxford Univ. Press, 1988).

83. Burns, *Roosevelt: The Soldier of Freedom*, 84.

84. Baer, *One Hundred Years of Seapower*, 148.

85. Burns, *Roosevelt: The Soldier of Freedom*, 349.

86. Ibid., 347.

87. Ibid., 353.

88. Ibid., 354-55.

89. Joel R. Davidson, *The Unsinkable Fleet* (Annapolis: Naval Institute Press, 1996), 22.

90. Friedman, *U.S. Destroyers*, 139.

91. Ibid.

92. The official files on the hybrid cruiser-carrier are detailed and extensive. See General Board memo to secretary of the Navy, "Proposed Fourth Endorsement," Sept. 14, 1931, attached to memo, "Design of Future Aircraft Carriers," Oct. 7, 1931; Chief of the Bureau of Aeronautics memo to the General Board, "Design of Future Aircraft Carrier," Nov. 12, 1931; Chief of the Bureau of Aeronautics memo to the Chief of Naval Operations, "Cruiser with Airplane Landing Deck, Study of," Sept. 19, 1934, all in General Board, file 420, RG 80, National Archives.

93. CINC, U.S. Fleet memo to CNO, "Cruiser with Airplane Landing Deck, Study of," General Board Files, 420-8, para. 1.

94. Norman Friedman, *U.S. Aircraft Carriers: An Illustrated Design History* (Annapolis: Naval Institute Press, 1983), 161-62.

95. Ibid.

96. Ibid.
97. See Norman Friedman, *U.S. Small Combatants: An Illustrated Design History* (Annapolis: Naval Institute Press, 1987), 31-32 for the World War I subchasers, 38-43 for the "eagle boats," and 48 for President Roosevelt's interest in subchasers in 1937.
98. Levine, *Politics of American Naval Rearmament,* 72.
99. *Hearings Before the General Board of the Navy, 1939* 1, "USS Hornet (CV8)," Jan. 19, 1939, 2, Naval Historical Center microfilm.
100. Heinrichs, *Threshold of War.*
101. See *Annual Report of the Commander-in-Chief, United States Pacific Fleet,* for the period July 1, 1940, to June 30, 1941. In folder "July-Dec. 1941," box 56, subject file 420, General Board, RG 80, National Archives.
102. "Ships Data, U.S. Naval Vessels," unpublished but official manuscript, vol. 3, 1942, Operational Archives, Naval Historical Center.
103. Secretary of the Navy, memo to All Bureaus of the Navy Department, "Statutory Limit for repairs and changes to naval vessels undertaken in a navy yard," Aug. 29, 1935, Op-23A-RSM, FS/L10-3(25)(350829), box 54, General Board file 420, RG 80, National Archives.
104. All these measures, and others, are listed in "Organization of the Navy Department," General Board Study, no. 446, RG 80, Naval Historical Center microfilm.
105. Buford Rowland and William Boyd, *U.S. Navy Bureau of Ordnance in World War II* (Washington, D.C.: GPO, 1953), 32-35, and 434 (for machine-tool manufacturers).
106. Ibid., 437-38.
107. Chief of Bureau of Navigation, memo to General Board, "Bill for the Reorganization of the Navy Department and for Amalgamation of certain Corps with the line as proposed by Congressman Vinson," Jan. 10, 1934, in "Organization of the Navy Department," General Board Study No. 446, Naval Historical Center microfilm.
108. Thomas C. Hone, "Navy Air Leadership: Rear Admiral William A. Moffett as Chief of the Bureau of Aeronautics," in *Air Leadership,* ed. Wayne Thompson (Washington, D.C.: Office of Air Force History, 1986), 109.
109. Henry M. Dater, "Tactical Use of Air Power in World War II: The Navy Experience," *Military Affairs* 14, no. 4, 193.
110. Eugene E. Wilson, *Slipstream* (New York: McGraw-Hill, 1950), 18.
111. R. A. Grossnick, *Dictionary of American Naval Aviation Squadrons,* vol. 1, App. 1 (Washington, D.C.: Naval Historical Center, 1995).

SEVEN

FDR AND THE ADMIRALS: STRATEGY AND STATECRAFT

Waldo Heinrichs

AS A DIPLOMATIC HISTORIAN feeling a bit out of place addressing a distinguished gathering in naval history, I am reminded of an awkward encounter with naval protocol experienced by Vice President Thomas Marshall in 1915, as told by FDR in his own words.

On the occasion of the vice president's visit to the San Francisco Exposition, he was honored with a reception on the flagship of the Pacific Fleet, attended by Roosevelt as assistant secretary of the Navy. The vice president had apparently not been given any instructions on how to come aboard a Navy ship.

He came alongside in the admiral's barge, climbed the gangway, and stepped over the rail to the grating—silk hat, frock coat, cigar in mouth, gloves in his left hand, cane in his right. Then the boatswain's pipe, four ruffles, and everyone at salute.

"The Star Spangled Banner" began and the vice president recognized his predicament. There was a moment of hesitation, but he then transferred the cane from right hand to left, took the cigar from his mouth, and with difficulty got his hat off. At the end of the national anthem, he started to put his hat on again (cane, cigar, gloves in his left hand) when the first gun went off. The whole works went two feet in the air.

A few days later, watching the whole scene in motion picture, the poor vice president turned to Roosevelt and said: "My God, if I looked like that I will never go on board another ship as long as I live."[1]

We know a great deal about Franklin Roosevelt and the Navy: about his love of ships and the sea, his rather too zestful administration of the Navy under Josephus Daniels, the pleasure he took in extensive cruising and traveling aboard American naval vessels, and his occasional wild idea about ship deployments, which horrified the admirals. A friend of the Navy he was, but admirals undoubtedly wished he were a less intrusive and more manageable friend.

I would like to venture beyond these connections to explore the interaction on substantive issues of national security of the President and the uniformed leadership of the Navy. That would seem to be a productive path to follow, for we are dealing with a president more than usually oriented toward international politics, and strongly inclined toward a military service which, facing and waging global war, was heavily dependent on him. We observe an intense interaction in a period of enormous change.

The most characteristic feature of FDR's relationship with his subordinates was his unorthodox administrative style. Complaints abound in the records: those who came to ask and tell had to listen; important diplomatic conversations went unrecorded; he secreted information; he embellished and otherwise contorted the truth; he played officials against each other; he shifted position from one caller to the next; bureaucratic lines of authority were subverted; and he generally sowed confusion. He seemed positively medieval in his methods, an enemy of modern, rational organization.

Yet Roosevelt only seemed to be prebureaucratic. He was by no means ignorant of modern administrative practice. Indeed, the Government Reorganization Bill of 1938, which he pressed on Congress without success, reflected his keen interest in making the federal government more efficient. The explanation for Roosevelt's idiosyncratic method of rule, it seems to me, lies elsewhere.

It was of course a matter of conserving power. His secrecy, obfuscation, compartmentalization of subordinates, and veiling of intentions enhanced the mystique of power and kept him aloof from the bureaucratic process rather than a prisoner of it.

In addition, this approach undoubtedly seemed necessary because of the extraordinary difficulty of forming policy in a world of heaving change and multiple threats, depending on an intelligence gathering system that was virtually nonexistent. Unsure of eventualities, FDR was the more inclined to abide by his native caution. Prudence dictated withholding decision until the right moment, until the variables clicked into place. Timing was everything. While waiting he might want to keep several courses of action, even contradictory ones, open. All the more important, then, was a shrouded, noncommittal posture.

Had Roosevelt laid bare his thoughts, it is a question whether the admirals would have been more enlightened. The professional naval mind, if I may hazard a guess, is primarily rationalist and quantifying, carefully ordered, and heavily engaged with doctrine and technology. The Roosevelt mind was political and disorderly, a cluster of facts, hypotheses, hunches, values, feelings, and perceptions. Analytical skill was not absent; visual imagery was probably strong. Somehow, according to Frances Perkins, these disparate faculties of FDR's mind worked together, winnowing, experimenting, integrating, weighing, classifying. From the process, policy evolved, stage by stage, responding to changing conditions and requirements. This was not a process, however effective, that was readily accessible to others. The president and the Navy would not easily communicate on matters of national security in the best of times and these were not the best of times.[2]

FDR's relations with the Navy as president may be divided into three main stages, each distinctly different in context and character from the others. The first stage, 1933 to 1938, may be described as the period of experimentation. FDR sought to protect the interwar Wilsonian system, such as it was, and to find ways of defining and limiting the reach of potential aggressors by diplomacy. The second stage, 1938 to 1942, was the period of engagement. Roosevelt, relying heavily on the Navy, moved to aid the victims of aggression, first by military aid, then deterrence and quasi war, and finally in global warfare. The third stage, 1943 to 1945, was the period of conquest, when the relations of Navy and president were integrated into a complex mechanism for direction of the war and the United States and its allies achieved crushing and decisive productive and military power. I will limit myself largely to the first two periods.

We can explain but not explain away the fact that the United States was appallingly unprepared for war in 1941 and that Roosevelt was ultimately—and in part directly—responsible. At the same time, it is incorrect to describe him as an isolationist, as if he regarded the threats developing in Europe and East Asia as irrelevant to American security. FDR was miles away from the mentality of a Burton K. Wheeler. He simply does not fit into neat compartments like "isolationist" or "internationalist."

During the period 1933-1938, Roosevelt's primary concern was national recovery from the Great Depression, not foreign affairs. The mood of the country was increasingly isolationist and a significant number of votes he needed for New Deal measures came from Progressives who were also isolationists. If not entirely aloof, Roosevelt was certainly detached from European diplomacy. Though apprehensive about Hitler's intentions and skeptical of British and French diplomacy, he was determined to stay out of trouble in Europe and East Asia.

That much is familiar, but we can go a step further. Barbara Farnham in a recent book persuasively argues that Roosevelt, though preoccupied and constrained at home, was not passive. Apprehensive about Hitler, yet unsure of his intentions, FDR tried one diplomatic device after another to pin him down and prevent another war and to test him out. Thus he had ideas about conciliation and disarmament, which in retrospect seem illusionary if not frivolous, as well as those looking toward nonmilitary coercion such as collective neutrality, embargo, and blockade.

None of these ideas worked, of course, but that is not really the point. As Farnham shows, Roosevelt was experimenting, seeking persistently to achieve his contradictory aims of preventing war and staying out of it, and he remained in that mode of policy until Munich gave him the answer regarding Hitler's intentions.[3]

Roosevelt once said, "When I don't know how to move, I stay put."[4] Staying put in the 1933-1938 period meant adhering to Wilsonian values, without collective security, respecting treaties, limiting arms, and above all seeking peace. If these were values of lessening relevance in the world of the thirties, they remained strongly attractive to the American people and FDR was determined to stick by them until some other course seemed imperative.

The United States Navy of 1933-1938 was strictly a treaty navy. For the London naval talks and conference of 1935-1936 the president insisted on maintaining existing qualitative and quantitative limitations and ratios, placing on Japan the onus of bringing the treaty era to an end. The Navy was underbuilt: the first Vinson building plan envisaged reaching treaty limits only in 1942. Even after the treaties, Roosevelt was reluctant to initiate a naval race, delaying construction of battleships while seeking evidence of Japan's building plans.

At the same time, the Navy did not starve. It received steady appropriations permitting prototype development in every category and new cruisers and destroyers in numbers to overcome severe deficiencies. Admiral William Standley, chief of naval operations, emphasized the importance for the American navy of the existing ratios. Steady, predictable, legitimated building plans were more likely to secure appropriations than unlimited international naval rivalry. On issues of size and shape, the president and the Navy, from their different perspectives, were on the same course.

The same applied in strategic planning. In the thirties, American plans for war in the Pacific became increasingly unrealistic. As Japanese aggression against China persisted and enlarged and the power of the American navy relative to the Japanese navy declined, the concept of steamroller advance by the fleet across the Pacific, meeting and defeating the Japanese fleet along the way, seemed more and more dubious. At the same time the Navy was loathe to shrink its mission and confine itself to defense of the Western Hemisphere.

One way to resolve the dilemma was to secure allies. In October 1937, Admiral Harry Yarnell, commander in chief of the Asiatic Fleet, put forward the idea of establishing a common front with nations whose territories were menaced by Japan—China, Britain, France, the Netherlands, and the Soviet Union—to encircle Japan and destroy its commerce with the outside world, on which its existence depended. Japan this way could be brought to its knees from afar, without a main fleet action.

The president, to whom Yarnell's letter was forwarded, was impressed. It fitted with his belief, he said, that since neither country could invade the home territory of the other, war between the United States and Japan would be decided by economic strength, with the United States of course the winner. He added that it accorded with his recent speech calling for a quarantine of aggressors.

He also inquired about the construction of a hybrid vessel— part picket boat, part cruiser, part seaplane tender—for intercepting Japanese commerce, apparently contemplating lines of these ships stretching across the shipping lanes. This was another of those Rube Goldberg ideas with which FDR seemed to delight in exasperating the Navy, to be sure, but it was not irrelevant to modern operations. Consider the U-boat wolf pack strung out in a line far into the Atlantic from the southern tip of Greenland to intercept convoys from North America, and the quarantine line of the Cuban Missile Crisis. Perhaps, too, FDR was prodding the Navy into forgetting Mahan for the moment and thinking about ways of conducting long-range defensive warfare. In the end, commerce interception occurred at home rather than at sea, taking the form in 1940-1941 of the embargo against Japan, with very large consequences.

The idea of coalition containment of Japan eventually became central to Roosevelt's Far Eastern policy. He probably had it in mind from the beginning. One purpose of opening relations with the Soviet Union was to check Japan. Similarly, he strove for Anglo-American solidarity at the London Naval Conference. It was typical of his foreign policy to isolate his adversaries by building alliances with their neighbors; thus the ABCD (American, British, Canadian, Dutch) coalition against Japan and the Grand Alliance against Germany. Shortly after the Yarnell letter came the *Panay* crisis, and shortly thereafter the secret Ingersoll mission to London to coordinate possible British-American fleet movements to Singapore and Hawaii, and then came visits by American warships to Australia and Singapore.

American policy toward Japan in the 1933-1938 period had more forceful implications than policy toward Europe, but these were mostly suggestive or conjectural or hidden. The public face of policy was nonprovocative. FDR considered East Asia less important than Europe; he regarded American interests there as less definitive, and more ambiguous, than did the Navy. Nevertheless, both he and the Navy from their different viewpoints found a promising alternative in the Yarnell idea and it worked its way into the war plans of 1938 and 1939. Both could agree on the need to keep a low profile in the Pacific.

Thus we find very little contention between FDR and the Navy in the period 1933-1938. The president was not intrusive, nor was the Navy contentious or disgruntled. It all seemed to be a smooth-running system, a model bureaucracy. Perhaps that was unfortunate given what was about to occur.

The following period, 1938-1942, was very different. In contrast to the detachment and tentativeness of the previous period, this was one of progressive engagement in world politics and war, from the decision after Munich to supply Britain and France with aircraft to the fall of France, Lend-Lease, escort of convoy, the oil embargo, Pearl Harbor, and Midway, to August and November 1942 and the first overseas assaults by American forces in the Solomons and North Africa. It was a time of unremitting crisis and shattering change. Now relations between the president and the Navy were difficult. The Navy was far more central to the president's purposes at this stage than was the Army, and FDR was at times demanding, insistent, and intrusive. As the occasion demanded, he became directly involved in plans, deployments, bases, and rules of engagement. Most admirals had no idea what the president's grand design was, if he had any, and how the Navy as a whole or any particular fleet fitted into it, and FDR provided little enlightenment. These circumstances and radical change, widening strategic perspectives and responsibilities, and competitive allocation of resources were bound to lead to disagreement and discord between the president and the Navy.

For Roosevelt, the Munich crisis finally clarified Hitler's intentions. Barbara Farnham is highly specific and convincing on this point. The dictator demonstrated his contempt for the procedures of compromise and peaceful settlement and for the rights and interests of others. A "wild man," to use FDR's words, he relied on force and his ambition knew no bounds.[5] Nazi air power, as FDR saw it, now seriously threatened Britain and France. Should they be conquered and the protection afforded by the Royal Navy be lost, the United States would stand alone in a totalitarian world. In those circumstances, the United States would face Nazi penetration of the Western Hemisphere. However, according to Farnham, in 1938 it was not so much in a territorial as in a procedural and ideological sense that the president marked Germany as an enemy: what mattered was Hitler's rejection of the basic norms of international intercourse, on which civilized and particularly democratic societies depended. One simply could not deal with Hitler.

Roosevelt took the first step in engagement with world politics by agreeing to build military airplanes for Britain and France in sufficient numbers to right the balance of air power and permit them to deter or defeat Hitler. The second step, taken at about the same time, was to provide a small but significant commodity loan to China to assist in its war against Japan. Despite these steps and the new perception of Hitler, American rearmament was only gradually increased. For example, the first of the four *Indiana*-class battleships was ordered in December 1938, but the last keel was not laid until 1940. Only one carrier was ordered. What the president wanted was early tangible military power delivered in Europe. Needless to say, the Army and Navy fought hard for a portion of the enlarging pie, with some success, but the president was determined here and in the coming months that the front-line nations receive enough military goods to make a difference, regardless of American military needs. Thereby he would transcend the contradiction between preventing a war and staying out of one.

The growing—and by June 1940 shocking—German threat led American military planning away from preoccupation with a Pacific war toward the Atlantic and Europe. Plans of 1939, reflecting the new importance of Europe and closer ties between the European Axis and Japan, took into account both spheres and single or multiple enemies. Plans of 1940-1941, encouraged by the president, called for concentration against Germany as the greater threat and defense in the Pacific; thus Rainbow 5, Plan Dog, and ABC-1. Clearly FDR and the admirals were heading in the same direction. For the Navy, every step of the way involved painful choices among competing imperatives.

In May 1940, in the face of evidence of impending Japanese advance into Southeast Asia, the president ordered the fleet to remain at Pearl Harbor as a deterrent. There it remained for 20 months, so credible a threat to the Japanese that they finally decided to destroy it. By 1940 the terms "deterrence" and "fleet to Hawaii" were practically synonymous, but little consideration had been given to what that meant in case of an extended stay. Indeed, the longer the fleet stayed, the harder it was to move it. Heavily engaged in expansion and training, it was not ready to venture westward. Its withdrawal or drawing down would give the impression of American weakening, which FDR would not permit. So it stayed tethered to its isolated, congested, yet alluring outpost, unable to take full advantage of the yards and schools on the mainland the way the Atlantic Fleet was using those on the East Coast in readying for action.

One can understand the frustration of the Pacific Fleet commanders, J. O. Richardson and Husband E. Kimmel. They had little idea of the president's larger design of an ABCD coalition, which in time would overpower Japan, but for the present was mostly symbolic. Yet the Pacific Fleet was not simply an inert symbol. One way or another, much of the fleet was put to work elsewhere. Consider the ships that weren't at Pearl Harbor on December 7: approximately one-quarter of the fleet had joined the Atlantic Fleet; a battleship and carrier were on the West Coast; two carriers were delivering planes to Midway and Wake, and most of the cruisers were escorting convoys across the Pacific, some of them "popping up" in Far Eastern ports, there noticed by the Japanese and contributing to Japan's sense of being encircled and its desire to break out.

Therefore, so long as the image of concentrated fleet power at Hawaii was maintained, as the president insisted, the Navy retained some flexibility in dispersing ships.

I suspect that what was most difficult for the Navy about the positioning of the fleet was the sense of loss of control and autonomy. On such questions the president broadened his circle of advisers to include the secretaries of war and state, and on the Atlantic redeployment question Churchill and the Royal Navy became involved. Particularly galling must have been outsider indifference to the Navy's professional requirements and doctrine. A similar sense of disempowerment would have resulted from problems arising from assignment of the Asiatic Fleet to ABDA (American, British, Dutch, Australian) command, the State Department's veto of withdrawal of American gunboats and marines from China, and the president's hands-on management of the Atlantic Fleet in the spring and summer of 1941. In this regard, the Navy was fortunate in having as Chief of Naval Operations Admiral Harold Stark. His political sensibilities and those of FDR helped ease the Navy into the era of integrated national security.

The spring of 1941 was a dismal time in the war against Hitler. The effort to supply Britain under Lend-Lease was threatened by staggering losses at the hands of German submarines and raiders. The British suffered a succession of defeats in the Middle East. The aims of Hitler and his seemingly invincible army remained, as I have argued elsewhere, unclear until early June.[6] American naval assets in the Atlantic were exceedingly limited. In this grim situation Roosevelt had two alternatives. The leadership of the Navy—Admirals Stark, Ingersoll, and Turner—argued that the United States should enter the Battle of the Atlantic now to sustain Britain and ensure control of the Atlantic, even though this undoubtedly meant war. Implementing British-American war plans, American destroyers should move to the United Kingdom to help protect the western approaches. Entry into war was justified by the supreme importance of controlling the Atlantic. The alternative was to do everything *short* of risking war to aid Britain and wait upon events.

Roosevelt chose the latter course, for the following reasons. In the first place, at the time, the number of destroyers that the American navy could contribute to the Battle of the Atlantic was not likely to make an appreciable difference in the outcome. Reinforcement of the Atlantic Fleet from the Pacific depended on whether Japan seemed intent on advancing further southward and was not fully authorized until June. In the second place, American engagement in the Battle of the Atlantic leading to war with Germany risked war with Japan under the obligations of the Axis alliance. That alliance, for the moment, was fully satisfying its objective of deterring the United States in both directions. In the third place, while American opinion was supportive of aid to Britain even at the risk of war, it was not likely to unite in support of an initiative that begged war.

So it was a matter of timing, but not only timing. It seems to me that the crisis of spring 1941 brought to the surface, from the core of Roosevelt's worldview, a hemispheric conception of American security. Some would argue that FDR's warnings of Nazi penetration of the Western Hemisphere were designed—whether sincerely or cynically—to dispel American complacency and open the way to stronger defense and more internationalist security policies. I would argue that his hemispheric feeling was instinctive and the foundation of his foreign-policy thinking. He was at heart a conservative nationalist like his cousin Theodore. A "map-minded" individual, as he said, he took the keenest interest in the insular stepping-stones to and from the Americas, inquiring about ownership of the Galapagos and islands south of Hawaii.[7] In 1941 his anxieties dwelt on German intentions toward the Cape Verdes, the Azores, Iceland, and Greenland, the latter not far from German-occupied Norway and the scene of German weather expeditions at Scoresby Sound. The appearance of German battleships in the western Atlantic, even off the Grand Banks, violated his fundamental sense of security no less than it did the Navy's.

I do not mean to suggest that Roosevelt was not an internationalist. He was both, but his world policies were not necessarily coextensive with his security policies. For the latter there was always a reserve, a citadel to defend. FDR regarded British survival as vital to American security but there was little beyond supplies that America could do to prevent an invasion if that was what Hitler chose to do in the spring of 1941. Thus I would regard FDR's interest in an American expedition to hold the Azores, in spite of

British assurances of protecting them, as evidence of his hemi-spheric concern: they would have to be defended if Britain went down, but they did not assist in the defense of Britain. FDR's later switch to Iceland as the focus of American interest, after Hitler's intent to invade the Soviet Union became clear, suggests the emergence of a broader policy, for Iceland was a necessary way station for supplying Britain and the Soviet Union, and thus for alliance formation and maintenance.

It was during this crisis-ridden spring of 1941 that FDR's most extensive intrusion into naval matters occurred. The problem was how the U.S. Navy could assist in the protection of shipping in the North Atlantic. Roosevelt met with the naval leadership repeatedly, even—and this was most unusual—with Admiral Ernest King, commander of the Atlantic Fleet, who came to Hyde Park to work out with the president detailed operational plans for his fleet.

Roosevelt proceeded far more cautiously than Admiral Stark had recommended. Setting aside for the time being escort of convoys, he ordered extended battleship, carrier, and cruiser patrols. These would report U-boats sighted but more importantly would establish an American naval presence in the western and central Atlantic that would mark out a broadened security zone for the Western Hemisphere. Instead of jumping into the Battle of the Atlantic, he proceeded in his own way, taking a step at a time eastward, reexamining developments and opportunities at each step. This approach fitted with Admiral King's. The latter was less than enthusiastic about placing his ships under British command and was determined to retain control and supervision over his fleet as it readied for battle.

Extended patrolling was a burden for the Atlantic Fleet but it posed a challenge for Hitler. Rather than risk an incident with the United States on the eve of his invasion of the Soviet Union, he withdrew U-boats from the western and central Atlantic. This sharply reduced sinkings in the summer, providing a credit in tonnage afloat that helped offset the terrible losses of 1942-1943.

This step-by-step process of cooperation between president and fleet commander continued through the summer as the United States prepared for escort of convoy—in the *western* Atlantic, Roosevelt weighing strategic and political factors, King establish- ing communications coordination with the British and operational capabilities. Once escort began and the rules of engagement were set, FDR turned to more pressing matters.

He remained deeply involved in military issues during the following year in the post–Pearl Harbor strategic revision, the appointment of Admiral King as commander in chief of the U.S. Fleet, the setting up of American and Allied mechanisms of decision making, and in pressing for offensive action in 1942, resulting in the North African and Guadalcanal landings, which fully engaged the United States in global conflict.

Once the targets, leadership, and mechanisms for victory were in place and American troops were in battle in both theaters, Roosevelt reverted to a more normal bureaucratic mode of leadership, somewhat similar to his more formal relationship in the first period. With two outstanding leaders, Admiral King and General Marshall, in place, he was less intrusive, though he did block King's attempt to take full control of the Navy's service bureaus. Generally, during the period of conquest, 1943-1945, he stayed aloof from the fray, intervening on occasion to umpire disputes or resolve impasses. Increasingly he was preoccupied with domestic politics and postwar planning. From the spring of 1944 onward, when the symptoms of progressive heart disease became apparent and his strength ebbed, he saw fewer people, read fewer papers, and gradually receded from hands-on manage- ment of government.

Roosevelt was no paragon of leadership; neither was he a cork bobbing on the waves. By examining his relations with the Navy in stages, we can see that his style of leadership varied not whimsi- cally but according to a highly volatile condition of world politics and shifting pressures as he saw them. Moving from one situation to the next, different faculties of mind and personality, and different techniques of management, came to bear.

Viewed this way, situationally, the contradictions and inconsistencies in our image of Roosevelt's relations with the Navy, and his foreign and security policies generally, can be somewhat modified and we can make better sense of his efforts to protect the nation in those years of great danger.

NOTES

1. Memorandum by FDR for his personal files, President's Personal Files, Franklin D. Roosevelt Library, Hyde Park, N.Y. This paper is mainly based on my book, *Threshold of War,* and essay, "The Role of the U.S. Navy," in ed., Dorothy Borg and Shumpei Okamoto *Pearl Harbor As History: Japanese-American Relations, 1931-1941* (New York: Oxford Univ. Press, 1973), 197-223.
2. Frances Perkins, *The Roosevelt I Knew* (New York: 1946), 161, 163.
3. Barbara Rearden Farnham, *Roosevelt and the Munich Crisis: A Study in Political Decision Making* (Princeton: Princeton Univ. Press, 1997).
4. As quoted in William L. Langer and S. Everett Gleason, *The Challenge to Isolation: The World Crisis of 1937-1941 and American Foreign Policy* (New York: Harper and Co., 1952), 597.
5. As quoted in Farnham, *Roosevelt and the Munich Crisis,* 156.
6. Heinrichs, *Threshold of War,* chaps. 1-4.
7. Gaddis Smith, "Forty Months: Franklin D. Roosevelt as War Leader, 1941-1945," *Prologue: Quarterly of the National Archives* 26, no. 3 (Fall 1994), 134.

EIGHT

ROOSEVELT AND CHURCHILL AND THE FIGHT FOR VICTORY AND STABILITY

Harold D. Langley

TEN DAYS AFTER WORLD WAR II BEGAN in Europe, President Franklin D. Roosevelt wrote to Winston S. Churchill, Great Britain's First Lord of the Admiralty, and invited Churchill to correspond with him. Personal and confidential letters could be sent about anything that Churchill or Prime Minister Neville Chamberlain thought the president should know about. Churchill responded with alacrity, and so a remarkable correspondence began and continued until Roosevelt's death in April 1945.[1]

In the beginning it was natural that the messages from Britain should be concerned with naval matters, but when Churchill became prime minister in May 1940 there was a great increase in the problems to be shared. France was on the verge of collapse as a result of the Nazi blitzkrieg. Churchill wanted the loan of 40 or 50 overage U.S. destroyers to fill the needs of the Royal Navy until new construction could be completed. He also needed several hundred of the latest aircraft, antiaircraft guns and ammunition, and steel and other materials. These would be paid for in dollars as long as the

British had the funds, but after that he hoped that Roosevelt would continue to ship the materiel. There was also the possibility of a German airborne assault on Ireland, so the visit of a U.S. Navy squadron to Irish ports would be a helpful deterrent. In addition, wrote Churchill, "I am looking to you to keep that Japanese dog quiet in the Pacific, using Singapore in any way convenient." It was an ambitious wish list to present on so short an acquaintance.[2]

For a president who was concerned about the extent of isolationist sentiment in the United States, it was a tall order indeed. Yet within four months the president got the legal authority to transfer 50 World War I destroyers to Great Britain in return for 99-year leases on air bases that would be built on British island possessions in the West Indies and in South America. Britain was also to use its influence to secure from Canada the right to build a similar base in Newfoundland. Churchill got his ships but Roosevelt had struck a hard bargain. In trading ships for bases to defend the Western Hemisphere the president disarmed his isolationist critics.[3]

When the British ran out of dollars to buy war materiel, Roosevelt succeeded in getting the Lend-Lease Bill through Congress in March 1941. This law authorized aid to countries whose defense was vital to the United States. Newly produced aircraft that were badly needed by the U.S. Army Air Forces were sent to Britain for "battle testing." But there were no visits of U.S. ships to Irish ports, and in the Pacific the American navy continued to be based at Pearl Harbor.[4]

As for the Japanese, both Roosevelt and Churchill hoped to keep them involved in negotiations in order to forestall any hostile moves. In the end it was Churchill who sent the battleship to Singapore.[5]

Building on the idea of helping Britain by stressing the concept of the defense of the Americas, in the spring of 1941 Roosevelt extended the security zone of the Western Hemisphere to the twenty-fifth meridian, or about midway between the bulge of Brazil and that of Africa. U.S. Navy and Coast Guard ships began patrolling this area. Under this arrangement American ships would report any enemy activity to the British. Agreements were signed with the Danes that led to the establishment of air bases in Greenland and the stationing of U.S. Marines in Iceland. Through the spring and summer of 1941 there was an increasingly close cooperation between the British and U.S. navies and between the Royal Air Force and the U.S. Army Air Forces. The Americans were also supplying British forces in Egypt directly by way of the Red Sea. Roosevelt was doing all that he thought he could do to help. Mindful of the isolationist sentiment of many Americans, he did not want to move too far ahead of public opinion.[6]

Meanwhile Hitler put pressure on Yugoslavia and the British urged that government to resist. There were rumors that the British had promised to give the city of Trieste to Yugoslavia after the war. To Churchill the president wrote that "it seems to me that it is much too early for any of us to make any commitments." Britain and the United States wanted to disarm all troublemakers, and in the interest of harmony to consider the possibility of reviving small states through plebiscites. In some cases preliminary plebiscites might be followed later by second or third plebiscites. "For example," wrote Roosevelt, "none of us know at the present time whether it is advisable in the interest of quiet conditions to keep the Croats away from the throats of the Serbs and vice versa." For the time being, the president wanted a statement from Churchill "that no postwar peace commitments as to territories, populations, or economies had been given." Roosevelt would then give a strong backing to such a statement.[7] Before anything of that nature could be done, Roosevelt and Churchill, accompanied by their military and naval advisors, held their first face-to-face meetings in Argentia Bay, Newfoundland, in August 1941.

Prior to the meeting, the British were advised that the president did not wish to discuss American entry into the war or postwar economic or territorial settlements. Nevertheless, at the first general meeting, Churchill asked for men, ships, planes, and tanks. He

wanted the United States to begin escorting convoys in the North
Atlantic. Evidence of mounting Japanese aggression made him
suggest that the United States, Great Britain, and the Soviet Union
warn Japan about moving troops to the Malay Peninsula or the
Dutch East Indies. The two leaders also discussed the allocation of
war material between the United States, Great Britain, and the Soviet
Union. The last power had been forced into the war as a result of the
German invasion of its territory in June. Neither the president nor
his military advisors were prepared to discuss specifics or make firm
decisions at that time. What was important was that the president
and the prime minister got along well, and Churchill was convinced
that the United States would soon be in the war.[8]

At the Argentia Bay meeting the president discussed the need
for a statement of principles that would inspire people and give
them some ideas about the postwar world. In his state of the union
message in January, the president had advanced his hopes for a
postwar world founded on four essential freedoms. These were
freedom of speech and religion, and freedom from fear and want.
He now wanted that vision to have an international dimension.
Among other things, it would be a justification for his secret
meeting with Churchill. After various drafts and suggestions, the
text of the Atlantic Charter was issued in a telegram that bore the
names of Churchill and Roosevelt. In it the two nations pledged not
to seek territorial or other aggrandizement; denounced territorial
changes that were not approved by the peoples concerned; affirmed
the rights of all peoples to choose their own form of government;
endorsed full economic collaboration between all nations; supported equal access to trade and raw materials; and looked forward
to a time of peace when all men in all lands could live out their lives
in freedom from fear and want.[9] The charter thus mentioned two
of the four freedoms and the other two could be said to be implied.

Following the conference, the increased activity of the U.S.
Navy in escorting British and neutral shipping as far as Iceland
resulted in clashes with German submarines. An attack on the

destroyer *USS Greer* in September led to Roosevelt's issuing a shoot-on-sight order to the Navy. An undeclared naval war with Germany began in the North Atlantic. In Washington the State Department demanded that something be done about the threatening movements of Japan in French Indochina. A decision was made to apply economic sanctions, including an embargo on the export of aviation oil to Japan. This action helped to accelerate the Japanese decision for war.[10]

Attacks by Japanese forces on Hawaii and the Philippines, and the declaration of war on the United States by Germany and Italy induced Churchill and his advisors to hurry to Washington for consultations. They were afraid that there would be a massive reallocation of war supplies to the Pacific. Instead they were surprised to learn that contingency plans already existed that provided that the United States would follow a Europe-first strategy in the event of a two-front war.[11]

While conferring with the president in Washington, Churchill was a guest in the White House. This close association was conducive to an atmosphere of informality and to frank exchanges of views. From this and subsequent meetings, there emerged a warm personal friendship. The two men were very different in their backgrounds, their work habits, and their approaches to military and naval affairs. Churchill had graduated from the Royal Military College at Sandhurst in 1895, and had subsequently served as a soldier, a war correspondent, a member of Parliament, the holder of the portfolios of minister of munitions, minister of war and air, and colonial secretary in various cabinets, as well as First Lord of the Admiralty for periods of time in both World Wars I and II. He felt that he knew a great deal about naval, military, and political matters. In World War I he overruled his military advisors and ordered the Gallipoli campaign, which resulted in a disaster and his retirement from office. He did not make that mistake again. In World War II he consulted and argued with his military and naval advisors. Reaching a conclusion was often a time-consuming and exhausting affair for everyone but Churchill. But when a decision had been made, everyone concerned was briefed on it. As a result, the British delegation presented a united front in their dealings with the Americans.[12]

Things were different in Washington. As a youth, Roosevelt had shown an interest in geography and in sailing. When he was 15 years old (two years after Churchill had graduated from Sandhurst) Roosevelt read Alfred T. Mahan's *The Influence of Sea Power Upon History,* and on his next birthday he received as a gift Mahan's work *The Interest of America in Sea Power.* These books helped to shape his ideas about sea power and for a time he considered becoming a naval officer. His parents disapproved that choice of a career, and as a dutiful son he accepted their judgment and went to Harvard. After graduation he studied law at Columbia Law School and became a member of a Wall Street law firm. His interest in naval matters was directed toward collecting early U.S. Navy prints and manuscripts. When his cousin Theodore became president, Franklin decided to enter politics. He seized the opportunity to serve as the assistant secretary of the Navy during World War I, and that experience, and his admiration for President Woodrow Wilson, played an important part in shaping Roosevelt's attitudes on naval and international affairs.[13]

In contrast with Churchill, Roosevelt did not have regular meetings with his chiefs of staff, but fitted them into his schedule when necessary. At the specific direction of the president, no written record was made of their discussions. When war came, and after the first Washington conference, better arrangements were necessary. The heads of the Navy, Army, and Army Air Forces, meeting as the Joint Chiefs of Staff, kept the President informed about all matters of policy.[14]

In an effort to improve his coordination and control, Roosevelt called from retirement Vice Admiral William D. Leahy, a former chief of naval operations and a diplomat, and installed him in the newly created position of Chief of Staff to the Commander in Chief.

Thereafter Leahy presided over the meetings of the Joint Chiefs, summarized the information they provided, and set forth the matters to be decided. With presidential approval, the Joint Chiefs then issued the orders that sent ships, planes, and men on their various missions. Because General George C. Marshall, the chief of staff of the Army, and General Henry Arnold, the head of the Army Air Forces, each had responsibilities for operations and plans, they had special access to the president, and this arrangement was formalized in February 1942.[15]

Beginning on January 23, 1942, and continuing on every Friday into the postwar years, the Joint Chiefs met with deputies of the senior commanders of the British armed forces who were assigned to Washington. As the Combined Chiefs of Staff, this body was responsible for a high degree of military coordination throughout the war.[16]

As time went on, Roosevelt came to rely increasingly on General Marshall's advice on military matters. In such a position of trust, Marshall was able to discourage any actions that he deemed imprudent. Marshall was also concerned about proper channels and constitutional prerogatives, and he briefed his superior, Secretary of War Henry L. Stimson, on plans and developments in the war. Stimson, in turn, held periodic lunches with Secretary of State Cordell Hull and Secretary of the Navy Frank Knox to keep them advised on what the president was doing. Roosevelt's executive order of October 18, 1941, designating Admiral Ernest J. King as both the commander in chief of the U.S. Fleet and as chief of naval operations, had the effect of making him independent of the secretary of the Navy in many ways. As an outward symbol of subordination, King attended the morning meetings of the bureau chiefs and heads of departments in the secretary's office, but Knox was excluded from matters relating to strategy and fleet operations. From King's point of view, the shore establishment and the support functions of the fleet were the proper domain of the secretary.[17]

Stimson's role in keeping the secretary of state advised about developments in the war tends to underscore the problems inherent in Roosevelt's penchant for personal diplomacy, and the way he pursued his vision of the postwar world. His contempt for orderly administration and written records of discussions made it difficult to determine the basis on which a decision had been reached. While Churchill tended to think simultaneously in military and political terms, and to balance long- and short-term goals, Roosevelt was apt to compartmentalize military and political affairs. He also tended to think globally and in idealistic and futuristic terms. The Atlantic Charter is one manifestation of that approach.[18]

Much to the disappointment of Marshall, Stimson, and others, Roosevelt and Churchill did not agree on the need to launch a cross-Channel attack on Nazi-occupied France as soon as possible. Churchill and his advisors considered such an operation premature and likely to result in heavy losses. Instead Churchill wanted to wear the Germans down through aerial bombardment and attacks on the periphery. If an invasion of France eventually became necessary, it then could be carried out with much smaller losses. Roosevelt, fearing the possibility of the collapse of the Soviet front, promised Foreign Minister Vyacheslav Molotov that American forces would be in action against Axis forces in Europe by the end of 1942. The only way that this promise could be kept was to agree to Churchill's proposal for an invasion of French Northwest Africa.

As Marshall and Stimson feared, the North African campaign inevitably led to the seizure of Sicily in July 1943, and to the invasion of Italy in September of that year. Further delays seemed to be in the cards. It was not until Roosevelt and Churchill had their first meeting with Stalin at Teheran, Iran, in November 1943 that things began to change. Stalin endorsed the American position on the need for a cross-Channel attack on German-held western Europe. He also indicated that he did not think that Anglo-American planners were serious about the invasion since they had not yet chosen a commander for the operation. Immediately after the Teheran meeting General Dwight D. Eisenhower was named as the supreme commander and the work of planning the invasion accelerated. Later the target date of May 1944 was chosen. Once the invasion was launched it was expected that the days of the Third Reich would be numbered. Meanwhile other problems demanded the attention of Roosevelt and Churchill and put strains on their relationship.[19]

At the first Washington conference in 1941, Roosevelt told Churchill that he favored the termination of India's colonial status in the British Empire. Churchill reacted strongly and at length against the idea, and the president never brought up the subject verbally again, but he did argue his case in his correspondence with the prime minister. Roosevelt had strong views on the necessity of ending colonialism. In his mind, the procedures put in place by the United States to give independence to the Philippine Islands in 1946 was the appropriate way to end colonialism. Churchill had other ideas.[20] Later, in November 1943, in a private meeting with Stalin at Teheran, the president expressed the desire to discuss India with him some day. He felt that the best solution would be reform from the bottom, "somewhat on the Soviet line." This comment surprised Charles Bohlen, the American foreign service officer who was acting as translator. He considered it "a striking example of Roosevelt's ignorance about the Soviet Union." Stalin responded that the Indian question was a complicated one involving different levels of culture and the lack of relations between castes. A reform from the bottom would be a revolution. Roosevelt did not pursue the matter.[21]

In March 1942 Churchill suggested that the Atlantic Charter ought not to be construed in a way that would deny to the Russians that portion of Poland that they occupied before the Nazi invasion of their homeland. Stalin wanted a treaty with Great Britain that would guarantee to the Soviet Union the territories it had taken from Poland, Finland, and the Baltic states. Roosevelt was opposed to this line of action.[22]

Later, in April 1944, King Peter of Yugoslavia wrote to Roosevelt and asked him to intervene so that the future of Yugoslavia, if not all the Balkan states, would not be decided without a common discussion and common guarantees by Great Britain, the United States, and the Soviet Union. In bringing this matter to Churchill's attention, Roosevelt said: "Personally I would rather have a Yugoslavia, but three separate states with separate governments in a Balkan confederation might solve many problems."[23]

In late May 1944 Churchill told Roosevelt that there were disquieting signs of a possible divergence of policy between the British and the Russians in regard to the Balkans and Greece. As a practical matter, Churchill suggested that the Soviet government take the lead in Rumanian affairs and that the British do the same in regard to Greece. He added that this proposal applied only to the wartime conditions, and that there was no attempt to carve up the Balkans into "spheres of influence." At the peace conference each of the three major powers would have rights and responsibilities in regard to the future of that area and for the "whole of Europe." Churchill hoped that the president would support this arrangement.[24]

Roosevelt did not endorse the proposal. He thought that the natural tendency would be for military governments to extend their authority into nonmilitary areas. This would lead to continuing differences between the British and the Russians and would ultimately result in spheres of influence. A better arrangement would be to establish "consultative machinery to dispel misunderstandings."[25] The prime minister did not find this advice to be helpful. When it became apparent that there would be no face-to-face meeting with Roosevelt to resolve this and other matters relating to the Russians, Churchill and Foreign Minister Anthony Eden flew to Moscow in October 1944 and conferred with Stalin. They came away with an agreement on the amount of influence each power would have in Rumania, Greece, Yugoslavia, Hungary, and Bulgaria. All this seemed like a case of carving out spheres of influence, as far as the Americans were concerned.[26]

Apparently some concern about the resurgence of isolationist sentiment after the war made Roosevelt wary about taking on occupation duties in Europe. In February 1944 the president told Churchill that he was unwilling to police France, Italy, or the Balkans. Such duties would naturally fall upon the troops that had liberated those areas. Churchill was not receptive to any changes. As late as June 2, 1944, the president again tried to change the postinvasion operational areas of the Allied forces in Europe so that the Americans would advance through Belgium, Holland, and northern Germany instead of across France. Roosevelt did not want the supply lines of American forces to be through France. But to accommodate the president on this issue would have involved a massive reorganization of the Normandy landing forces and a delay in launching the invasion.[27]

Churchill visualized a future in which Anglo-American wartime cooperation would eventually grow to the point that both Americans and British would share a common citizenship. Roosevelt never shared this view, and by the end of 1943 he had begun to take steps to disassociate himself from any perceptions of an Anglo-American unity in all matters. This attitude led to Roosevelt's inviting Chiang Kai-shek to a meeting in Cairo that had originally been slated for Anglo-American discussions. Roosevelt and Churchill held their first meeting with Stalin in Teheran, Iran, in November 1943. At this meeting Roosevelt refused to stay at the British legation. It was at Teheran that Stalin supported the American position in regard to the cross-Channel attack. By this time political questions were demanding increased attention. In 1945 Churchill wanted a meeting with Roosevelt at Malta in order to coordinate Anglo-American policy prior to the meeting with Stalin at Yalta. Roosevelt did not want Stalin to think that the British and Americans were ganging up on the Russians, so the meeting at Malta was brief and dealt mostly with military matters.[28]

For Churchill, the lowest point in the Anglo-American wartime alliance was at Yalta, where the president, who was the chairman of the meeting, tried to act as a mediator in regard to British and Soviet ideas of postwar arrangements. At Yalta, Roosevelt and Stalin reached a private agreement on the Far East that did not involve Churchill.[29]

Other examples might be cited to show differences between Roosevelt and Churchill over political decisions that would affect the postwar world, and the president's inability to block policies of which he disapproved. Roosevelt was also tired, ill, and often lonely. He needed reliable help in sorting through the problems and considering the options. Earlier in the war, Harry Hopkins was one of the president's most trusted advisors. Churchill also had a high opinion of Hopkins, and the American had a good relationship with Stalin.[30] But in January 1944 Hopkins became seriously ill and was hospitalized. He was out of commission for seven months. When he returned, the old close association with the president could not be reconstituted. Hull was also ill and preparing to retire. Every senior person with experience in foreign affairs had been eliminated from policymaking.[31]

For a time the president had toyed with the notion of the Four Policemen—the idea that Britain, the United States, China, and the Soviet Unionmight keep peace in the developing world while the fledgling nations there were prepared for independence.[32] By 1945, this seemed an unrealistic goal. The immediate need was to keep the Soviet Union in the war, to use its armed might to help subdue Japan, and to induce the Russians to participate in the work of the United Nations and the postwar peace treaties. The American people also had to be inspired to endorse U.S. participation in the United Nations and in the process of determining the shape of the postwar world. So, despite the flawed diplomacy, unfortunate developments, and the distortion of the Atlantic Charter, Roosevelt continued to speak to the American public of the Four Freedoms until the end of his days.[33] The State Department developed its postwar positions on the diplomatic record and the public statements of the president. When Roosevelt died, Harry S. Truman promised the American people that he would carry out his predecessor's policies.[34]

NOTES

1. Francis L. Loewenheim, Harold D. Langley, and Manfred Jones, eds., *Roosevelt and Churchill: Their Secret Wartime Correspondence* (New York: Saturday Review Press/E. P. Dutton, 1975), preface.
2. Ibid., 94-95; Warren F. Kimball, ed., *Churchill and Roosevelt: The Complete Correspondence*. 3 vols. (Princeton: Princeton Univ. Press, 1984), i: 37-38.
3. Loewenheim, Langley, and Jones, *Roosevelt and Churchill*, 95-96, 108-9, 112-13; Kimball, *Churchill and Roosevelt,* 1: 38-40, 54-60, 65-69; William L. Langer and S. Everett Gleason, *The Challenge of Isolation, 1937-1940* (New York: Harper & Brothers, 1952), 742-76; David Reynolds, "Lord Lothian and Anglo-American Relations, 1939-1940," *Transactions of the American Philosophical Society* 73, pt. 2 (1983): 24-29. For a recent interpretation of the destroyer-base deal, see Robert Shogan, *Hard Bargain: How FDR Twisted Churchill's Arm, Evaded the Law, and Changed the Role of the American Presidency* (New York: Scribners, 1995). A popular account of the deal is in Philip Goodhart, *Fifty Ships That Saved the World: The Foundation of the Anglo-American Alliance* (Garden City, N.Y.: Doubleday & Co., 1965).
4. Loewenheim, Langely, and Jones, *Roosevelt and Churchill,* 122-25; Kimball, *Churchill and Roosevelt,* 1: 102-11, 120; Warren F. Kimball, *The Most Unsordid Act: Lend Lease, 1939-1941* (Baltimore: Johns Hopkins Univ. Press, 1969).
5. Kimball, *Churchill and Roosevelt,* 1: 74, 135-37, 192-95, 225; Waldo Heinrichs, *Threshold of War: Franklin D. Roosevelt and American Entry into World War II* (New York: Oxford Univ. Press, 1988), 63-145; Jonathan G. Utley, *Going to War With Japan, 1937-1941* (Knoxville: Univ. of Tennessee Press, 1985), 101-37.
6. Kimball, *Churchill and Roosevelt,* 1: 166, 172-74, 183, 192-96, 198, 203, 207, 209-11, 225; Patrick Abbazia, *Mr. Roosevelt's Navy: The Private War of the U.S. Atlantic Fleet, 1939-1942* (Annapolis: Naval Institute Press, 1975), 151-212; Stetson Conn, Rose C. Engleman, and Byron Fairchild, *Guarding the United States and its Outposts* (Washington: U.S. Government Printing Office (GPO), 1962), 442-507; Samuel I. Rosenman, *Working With Roosevelt* (New York: Harper & Brothers, 1952), 266.
7. Loewenheim, Langley, and Jones, *Roosevelt and Churchill,* 149-51; Kimball, *Churchill and Roosevelt,* 1: 221-22.

8. Loewenheim, Langley, and Jones, *Roosevelt and Churchill*, 153-54; Kimball, *Churchill and Roosevelt*, 1: 227; Forrest C. Pogue, *George C. Marshall: Ordeal and Hope, 1939-1942* (New York: Viking Press, 1966), 142-45; Thomas B. Buell, *Master of Sea Power: A Biography of Fleet Admiral Ernest J. King* (Annapolis: Naval Institute Press, 1980), 142-45; Winston S. Churchill, *The Second World War: The Grand Alliance* (Boston: Houghton Mifflin Co., 1950), 427-45; Theodore A. Wilson, *The First Summit: Roosevelt and Churchill at Placentia Bay, 1941* (Boston: Houghton Mifflin Co., 1969); Robert Dallek, *Franklin D. Roosevelt and American Foreign Policy, 1932-1945* (New York: Oxford Univ. Press, 1979), 282-85.

9. Loewenheim, Langley, and Jones, *Roosevelt and Churchill*, 154-55; Kimball, *Churchill and Roosevelt*, 1: 227-28; Churchill, *The Grand Alliance*, 433-44.

10. Abbazia, *Mr. Roosevelt's Navy*, 223-31, 255-341; Dallek, *Franklin D. Roosevelt and American Foreign Policy*, 287-89, 292, 299-311; Heinrichs, *Threshold of War*, 159-69, 176-218; Utley, *Going to War With Japan*, 138-82.

11. Churchill, *The Grand Alliance*, 641-43, 662-68; Dallek, *Franklin D. Roosevelt and American Foreign Policy*, 318-24; Pogue, *George C. Marshall: Ordeal and Hope*, 263-88.

12. Loewenheim, Langley, and Jones, *Roosevelt and Churchill*, 14-16.

13. Ibid., 16-20.

14. Ibid., 25-26; Dallek, *Franklin D. Roosevelt and American Foreign Policy*, 532.

15. Loewenheim, Langley, and Jones, *Roosevelt and Churchill*, 25; William D. Leahy, *I Was There* (New York: Whittlesey House, 1950), 96-97; Pogue, *George C. Marshall: Ordeal and Hope*, 298-300.

16. Loewenheim, Langley, and Jones, *Roosevelt and Churchill*, 24; Churchill, *The Grand Alliance*, 686-88.

17. Henry L. Stimson and McGeorge Bundy, *On Active Service in Peace and War* (New York: Harper & Brothers, 1948), 332, 362-63; Buell, *Master of Sea Power*, 233-34.

18. Arthur Layton Funk, *The Politics of Torch: The Allied Landings and the Algiers Putsch, 1942* (Lawrence: Univ. of Kansas Press, 1974), 29-32, 65-87; Richard W. Steele, *The First Offensive, 1942: Roosevelt, Marshall, and the Making of American Strategy* (Bloomington: Indiana Univ. Press, 1973), 46-182; Churchill, *The Grand Alliance*, 699-706.

19. U.S. Department of State, *The Conferences at Cairo and Teheran, 1943* (Washington: GPO, 1961), 533-52; 565-68; Loewenheim, Langley, and Jones, *Roosevelt and Churchill*, 395-96; Kimball, *Churchill and Roosevelt*, 2: 606-7, 610-11, 613; Gerhard L. Weinberg, *A World At Arms: A Global History of World War II* (New York: Cambridge Univ. Press, 1994), 628-29; Keith Eubank, *Summit at Teheran: The Untold Story* (New York: William Morrow and Co., 1985), 258-62, 279-83, 303-13, 323-24; Dwight D. Eisenhower, *Crusade in Europe* (New York: Doubleday & Co., 1948), 206-8.

20. U.S. Department of State, *The Conferences at Washington 1941-1942 and Casablanca 1943* (Washington: GPO, 1968) passim; Loewenheim, Langley, and Jones, *Roosevelt and Churchill*, 190-92; Kimball, *Churchill and Roosevelt*,

1: 373-79, 388-89, 394-96, 402-4, 444-49; Churchill, *The Second World War: The Hinge of Fate* (Boston: Houghton Mifflin Co., 1950), 209-21; Christopher Thorne, *Allies of a Kind: The United States, Britain and the War Against Japan, 1941-1945* (New York: Oxford Univ. Press, 1978), 233-51.

21. Charles E. Bohlen, *Witness to History, 1929-1969* (New York: W.W. Norton & Co., 1973), 140-41; U.S. Department of State, *The Conferences at Cairo and Teheran 1943*, 485-86.

22. Loewenheim, Langley, and Jones, *Roosevelt and Churchill*, 186; Kimball, *Churchill and Roosevelt*, 1: 394, 490, 557, 559-60.

23. Loewenheim, Langley, and Jones, *Roosevelt and Churchill*, 497-98; Kimball, *Churchill and Roosevelt*, 3: 132-33.

24. Loewenheim, Langley, and Jones, *Roosevelt and Churchill*, 502-3; Kimball, *Churchill and Roosevelt*, 3: 153-54.

25. Loewenheim, Langley, and Jones, *Roosevelt and Churchill*, 526-27; Kimball, *Churchill and Roosevelt*, 3: 177.

26. Loewenheim, Langley, and Jones, *Churchill and Roosevelt*, 502-3, 583-84; Kimball, *Churchill and Roosevelt*, 3: 153-54, 177, 178-80, 181-82, 200-1, 348-51, 353; Churchill, *The Second World War: Triumph and Tragedy* (Boston: Houghton Mifflin Co., 1953), 226-34.

27. Loewenheim, Langley, and Jones, *Roosevelt and Churchill*, 456-57, 501-4; Kimball, *Churchill and Roosevelt*, 3: 146-47, 150, 159.

28. Thorne, *Allies of a Kind*, 103, 507-9, 676; Loewenheim, Langley, and Jones, *Roosevelt and Churchill*, 38-39, 60-63, 653-57; Kimball, *Churchill and Roosevelt*, 3: 469-70, 477-78, 479, 484, 486, 488-89, 491, 493-96, 501-3, 521-26; Eubank, *Summit at Teheran*, 486-89.

29. Kimball, *Churchill and Roosevelt*, 3: 527; Bohlen, *Witness to History*, 196-99.

30. James MacGregor Burns, *Roosevelt: The Soldier of Freedom, 1940-1945* (New York: Harcourt Brace Jovanovich, 1970), 73, 112, 182, 221, 230-31, 236, 244.

31. Dallek, *Franklin D. Roosevelt and American Foreign Policy*, 502-3; Beatrice Bishop Berle and Travis Beal Jacobs, eds., *Navigating the Rapids, 1918-1971: From the Papers of Adolf A. Berle* (New York: Harcourt Brace Jovanovich, 1973), 584-86.

32. Dallek, *Franklin D. Roosevelt and American Foreign Policy*, 342, 389-90, 434, 482.

33. Ibid., 510-28; Rosenman, *Working With Roosevelt*, 497.

34. Harry S. Truman, *Memoirs: Year of Decisions* (Garden City, N.Y.: Doubleday & Co., 1955), 9.

NINE

ROOSEVELT AND LEAHY: THE ORCHESTRATION OF GLOBAL STRATEGY

Paul L. Miles

NEARLY 35 YEARS AGO, Kent Roberts Greenfield observed that it was largely due to Franklin Roosevelt's exercise of his authority as commander in chief that the United States developed "an American strategy appropriate to a global two-front war, one that brought almost simultaneously victory over both Japan and Germany."[1] In light of recent scholarship, particularly that occasioned by the fiftieth anniversary of World War II, one implication of Greenfield's statement rings even more true: that is, the key to understanding Roosevelt's approach to the conduct of war is his search for a framework of strategy that would bring American military and economic power to bear at an array of decisive points around the globe.

In offering this judgment, it is not necessary to infer from the record. Roosevelt can speak for himself. He signaled his approach to strategic planning as early as January 1941. At a time when his diplomatic and military advisers were speculating about the connection between Japanese moves in the Far East and German aggression in Europe, the president set forth his views in a message to the United States ambassador in Tokyo: "We must recognize that the hostilities in Europe, in Africa, and in Asia are all parts of a single world conflict. . . . Our strategy must be a global strategy."[2]

After the attack on Pearl Harbor, the challenge of waging war on disparate battlefronts became a recurrent topic in the president's public statements. He introduced this theme in February 1942, when he devoted a fireside chat to a discussion of the geographical scope of the conflict. "This war is a new kind of war," he said. "It is different . . . not only in its methods and weapons but also in its geography. It is warfare in terms of every continent, every island, every sea, and every air lane in the world."[3]

Despite repeated efforts to illustrate the interdependent nature of operations in a global conflict, Roosevelt as late as September 1943 found it necessary to elaborate on the character of the war. In a message to Congress, he observed: "People continually make the mistake of trying to divide the war into several watertight compartments. . . . You even hear talk of the 'air war' as opposed to the 'land war' or the 'sea war.' . . . It is all one war, and it must be governed by one basic strategy."[4]

No one was more energetic in reiterating Roosevelt's admonition than Admiral William D. Leahy, the president's wartime chief of staff. When Leahy addressed the Combined Chiefs of Staff (CCS) at the Washington Conference in May 1943, he took his cue from the commander in chief. The Combined Chiefs, he argued, should bring a global perspective to the task of developing strategy for the Anglo-American coalition: "Our two principal enemies, widely separated and constituting threats to our home theaters that differ in imminence and gravity, present problems that are inextricably interrelated. . . . Any major course of action against one enemy has a direct effect upon the timing, scope, and objective of action against the other. The global concept must, therefore, be kept constantly in mind."[5]

William Leahy remains the least known of that remarkable band of lieutenants who assisted Franklin Roosevelt in the conduct of World War II. In comparison with other members of the Joint Chiefs of Staff (JCS), notably George Marshall and Ernest King, and in contrast to larger-than-life commanders in the field like Dwight Eisenhower and Douglas MacArthur, Leahy remains an elusive personality, one who seldom emerges from the footnotes of history. Let me reintroduce this extraordinary sailor-statesman.

Leahy was the one member of Roosevelt's inner circle of military advisers whose public life bridged the nineteenth and twentieth centuries. A graduate of the United States Naval Academy, Class of 1897, he was aboard the battleship *Oregon* when she raced from the Pacific to the Atlantic to employ her guns against the Spanish squadron at Santiago de Cuba.[6]

Leahy's career during the next 20 years was not markedly different from that of other naval officers of his generation. But there was one exception: in 1915 he was given command of the *Dolphin,* the secretary of the Navy's dispatch boat, an assignment that brought him into contact with Assistant Secretary of the Navy Franklin Roosevelt, who occasionally commandeered the *Dolphin* for both business and pleasure.

After heading the Bureau of Ordnance at the end of the 1920s, Leahy in the following decade served successively as chief of the Bureau of Navigation, Commander Battleships, and Commander Battle Force before being named chief of naval operations in January 1937. When Leahy retired from active duty in August 1939, the president awarded him the Distinguished Service Medal with a citation praising his leadership of the Navy "during a period when the greatest peacetime expansion in history was reaching its peak."

Leahy's respite from public life was brief. With the outbreak of war in Europe, Roosevelt called upon him to serve as governor of Puerto Rico at a time when American national security was being redefined in terms of hemispheric defense. Then, in a move that thrust Leahy into the forefront of United States foreign affairs,

Roosevelt appointed him ambassador to the French government in Vichy. In this post, Leahy endeavored to ensure some measure of neutrality on the part of the Vichy regime and prevent the French fleet and overseas bases from falling into the hands of the Axis.[7]

In the spring of 1942, Roosevelt recalled Leahy from France and subsequently appointed him chief of staff to the commander in chief, a position for which there was no precedent. The president took this step amid an atmosphere of crisis. On July 22, the day that Leahy's appointment was the lead article in the press, front pages also reported the Russian army's desperate defense of Rostov and alarming news from the War Shipping Administration. Enemy submarines had sunk more Allied ships during the second week in July than in any week since the war began. "The military situation of the United Nations," proclaimed the *Times* of London, "is probably now graver than at any time since the summer of 1940."[8]

July 1942 was also a time marked by dissension on the home front. As the military situation deteriorated, longstanding dissatisfaction with direction of the war effort intensified. The *New York Herald-Tribune* captured the mood of much of the public when it editorialized: "The American people are experiencing a growing sense of frustration and dismay over the apparent inability to bring our great strength to bear effectively at any point in this critical juncture."[9]

With these developments as a backdrop, it is not surprising that commentators—American and British alike—sought to interpret Leahy's appointment as an omen of dramatic initiatives. Some newspapers linked Leahy's new assignment with "ever-recurring talk about a second front." According to the *Herald-Tribune*, Leahy presumably knew "more than any one else in the United States about the prospects for success of an invasion of France." In London, the *Times* interpreted the admiral's appointment as a "visible sign" of the American government's recognition of the "supreme importance of the sea in the conduct of the war." The surge in Allied shipping losses pointed to one conclusion: "Command of the seas should be the first objective. . . . And the presence of Admiral Leahy at Mr. Roosevelt's right hand will be a token that it is to be kept continuously in view."[10]

The president himself attempted to play down expectations. When Roosevelt announced Leahy's appointment at a White House press conference, reporters pressed for details. "Can you tell us what the scope of his office will be?" asked one. Roosevelt replied that Leahy would be chief of staff to the commander in chief. "Will he have a staff of army, navy, and air force officers under him?" asked another. The president said that he did not have the "foggiest idea" and that the question had "nothing to do with the price of eggs." Roosevelt, described by one reporter as "patiently demonstrating impatience," also denied any connection between Leahy's appointment and rumors that Churchill and American officials were meeting to confirm plans for a second front. A reporter asked, "Does the appointment of Leahy mean that the commander in chief will take a more active part in the strategy of the war?" The president laughed and said that was impossible. Leahy's own description of the scene mirrored the accounts of journalists: "The President was cagey, as he always was in dealing with the newsmen, and did not tell them very much."[11]

In retrospect, the columnist Walter Lippmann appears to have provided the most perceptive commentary on Leahy's appointment. Lippmann viewed the president's announcement not as an omen of strategic initiatives but as a solution to organizational problems: "a response to the task of equipping the commander in chief with resources that will enable him to make sound decisions in a global and three-dimensional war." The president, Lippmann wrote, "needed assistance" in evaluating strategic plans from perspectives "that are much wider—because they include vast political and social factors—than the operational staffs can be expected to pass upon."[12]

Lippmann also foresaw more effective control of the military departments. Comparing Roosevelt with Lincoln during the early years of the Civil War, the columnist noted Roosevelt's "strong disposition . . . to decide too many things that the commander in chief should not have to decide." The president, "acting now and then on tidbits of information and his intuition," had attempted to be not only his own secretary of state but also his own secretary of the Navy. "With Admiral Leahy at his right hand, we may hope for better days."[13]

"This is an order from the President of the United States and is not a matter for discussion," declared Leahy in September 1942, when he intervened to resolve a contentious issue before the Board of Economic Warfare (BEW). In making this statement, Leahy demonstrated his determination to enforce Roosevelt's policy by invoking, if necessary, the president's authority as chief executive. But Leahy's appearance before the BEW held additional meaning. Within two months of assuming his new post in the White House, the president's chief of staff had moved beyond the boundaries of military affairs to become involved in the diplomatic and economic dimensions of the American war effort.[14]

Leahy's initial concept of his role as the president's senior military assistant appears to have been a conventional one. He viewed his functions in terms of the traditional duties of a chief of staff in a naval command. In his memoir of the war years, he wrote, "I do not recall that Roosevelt recommended the actual title 'Chief of Staff,' but the duties that he outlined, such as daily contact with the three branches of the armed services, the reading of reports and giving him summaries and digests, added up to the kind of post that we referred to in the Navy as a 'chief of staff.'"[15]

Leahy apparently did not anticipate the part that he would play as a member of the JCS or the CCS.[16] Moreover, there is little evidence that he had in mind the tasks that he would fulfill in the field of diplomacy. Nevertheless, by December 1942, he was relaying Roosevelt's instructions to the State Department, drafting messages to the British prime minister, and representing the president in meetings with Allied envoys.[17]

It is doubtful that the president himself possessed any clearer picture of Leahy's exact role. In private conversation, Roosevelt had said that Leahy would assist in "coordinating the operations of the armed forces." This description of Leahy's role as a coordinator implied broad responsibilities, at least in the military sphere, but Roosevelt's public statements had been ambiguous. Indeed, his description of Leahy's duties as "legwork" for the commander in chief suggested a circumscribed mission. Still, it was the president himself who accelerated the process whereby Leahy became more involved in the coordination of grand strategy.[18]

One week after Roosevelt had intimated a narrow charter for his chief of staff, he began to enlist Leahy's assistance in the fields of mobilization and diplomacy. In late July, Roosevelt requested Leahy's views on the industrialist Henry Kaiser's proposal to construct large transport planes for the armed forces.[19] In September, Roosevelt recruited Leahy to work with Harry Hopkins in drafting replies to messages from Winston Churchill that dealt with the invasion of North Africa and lend-lease convoys to Russia.[20] And by the end of the month, Leahy was meeting with the president and the director of the budget to discuss manpower issues.[21]

Just as it is hazardous to draw a fine line between the role of the president as chief executive and his responsibilities as commander in chief, so also it is difficult to distinguish between Leahy's multiple roles. Leahy served at the crossroads of policy and strategy, and his manifold functions reflected the degree to which his military duties as chief of staff merged with the broader responsibilities of a presidential assistant in time of war. His role was to assist Roosevelt not only with the coordination of the ends and means of military strategy but also with the orchestration of grand strategy in a global war.

Notwithstanding the diversity of Leahy's tasks, there is no excuse for being unclear about his principal duty. It was, in his own words, "the maintenance of daily liaison between the President and the Joint Chiefs of Staff." As he explained, "it was my job to pass on to the Joint Chiefs . . . the basic thinking of the President on all war plans and strategy. In turn, I brought back from the Joint Chiefs a consensus of their thinking."[22]

Leahy's terse description fails to convey the full scope and complexity of his responsibilities. As the president's representative to the JCS, Leahy played an instrumental role in harmonizing military courses of action with the political aims of the commander in chief. Conversely, as the Joint Chiefs' liaison with the president, Leahy frequently tempered Roosevelt's notions of global strategy with the reality of military necessity and logistical constraints.

What was Leahy's own outlook on the relationship between policy and strategy? Although not a student of military thought, Leahy viewed strategic issues with a perspective that exemplified Clausewitz's fundamental thesis that "war is not an independent phenomenon, but the continuation of politics by different means."[23] For Leahy, the concept that war was an instrument of policy was axiomatic. In his writings and public statements, the word *policy* punctuates his account of the American war effort. Rather than dwelling upon problems of military strategy, Leahy frequently underlined the fundamentals of policy. For example, when he recorded the guidance that was issued in planning for the Allied occupation of Sicily, he wrote, "the President approved, with some changes, of course, a message I drafted for General Eisenhower outlining American policy in this matter." When he described the crux of the debate over strategy at the Washington Conference in 1943, he stated, "Churchill appeared . . . to carry his insistent campaign to preserve the British Empire to a point where it might not be in full agreement with the President's fundamental policy to defeat Hitler as quickly as possible." After the war, when the University of Wisconsin invited him to address the faculty on the role of the high command, Leahy chose not to examine strategic issues per se but to discuss "United States Policy in World War II."[24]

Leahy's loyalty to Roosevelt's policy explains the pattern of his initiatives in the proceedings of both the Joint Chiefs and the

Combined Chiefs. The minutes of the JCS indicate that Leahy was not as aggressive in debates over military strategy as were Marshall and King. When he joined the discussions, he often assumed the role of moderator. But it would be misleading to portray Leahy as merely a mediator between the chiefs of services or as just an arbiter of Anglo-American differences. Although he usually took an indirect approach, he was instrumental in clarifying—and enforcing—the policy of the commander in chief. Let me illustrate by reference to two of the fabled "command decisions" of the war: first, the decision for Operation Torch, the invasion of North Africa; and second, the even more fundamental decision of global strategy—the decision capsulized in the slogan Germany First.

Leahy presided for the first time at a meeting of the CCS on July 30, 1942, just days after Hopkins, Marshall, and King had concluded the negotiations in London that laid the groundwork for the North African landings. In his opening statement, the president's chief of staff expressed his understanding of Roosevelt's and Churchill's agreement on the course of Anglo-American strategy: "Both the President and the Prime Minister now firmly believe that the decision to undertake Torch has . . . been reached and that all preliminary arrangements are proceeding as rapidly as possible in order that the operation may be undertaken at the earliest possible date." It was Leahy's position that the concept of an invasion of North Africa was no longer at issue. Rather, the main item on the agenda was the development of operational plans for the campaign.[25]

Although the British representatives were ready to proceed with preparations for the landings, Marshall reneged. The Army's chief of staff initiated a last-ditch maneuver to defer detailed planning for Torch. Marshall stated that it was not clear to him that the president understood that a decision to mount Torch was tantamount to a decision to abandon Operation Roundup, the invasion of western Europe that had been projected for 1943. Consequently, the War Department was proceeding with a study "of all implications of

Torch." King, following Marshall's lead, also expressed the belief that the president and the prime minister "had not yet reached agreement to abandon Roundup in favor of Torch."[26]

In arguing that a final decision for Torch was yet to be made, Marshall and King cited the ambiguous wording of CCS 94, the document that summarized the decisions of the London Conference. Instead of recording an irrevocable commitment to proceed with the North African landings, CCS 94 made preparations for Torch contingent on a formal decision to abandon Roundup, and in turn, linked the disposition of Roundup with the situation on the eastern front.[27]

Leahy acted quickly to dispel any doubt about Roosevelt's position. Rather than engaging in a debate over the meaning of CCS 94, Leahy announced that he would "tell the President that a definite decision was yet to be made." The Joint Chiefs did not have to wait very long for a definite decision. After meeting with Leahy on the evening of July 30, Roosevelt terminated the deliberations over Torch with an announcement that was communicated in writing to the JCS: "The President stated very definitely that he, as Commander-in-Chief, had made the decision that Torch would be undertaken at the earliest possible date. He considered that this operation was now our principal objective and the assembly of means to carry it out should take precedence over other preparations."[28]

While serving as ambassador to France, Leahy had endorsed the basic tenet of American strategy for a two-ocean war: the decision to aim first for the defeat of Germany. This concept meant, in Leahy's words, that the Allies would "concentrate first on administering total defeat to the Axis powers in Europe, while conducting a campaign of attrition against the Japanese." At the same time, Leahy sided with the Navy's planners in arguing that the Germany First strategy did not mean that the United States should postpone indefinitely major offensive operations against Japan. Among other reasons, the president's chief of staff understood that American political interests dictated a commitment to the Pacific that deviated from the pristine implementation of Germany First proposed by Churchill and the British chiefs of staff. At the Washington Conference in 1943, Leahy stated his views in unambiguous terms: "The Pacific could not be neglected; it was too vital to the United States. Immediate action was necessary."[29]

Leahy's attention to the Pacific theater revealed, in particular, his understanding of the role that China played both in American strategy for the defeat of Japan and in Roosevelt's plans for the postwar world. In the summer of 1942, when military considerations militated against the shipment of additional munitions to the Chinese, Leahy reminded the Joint Chiefs of broader, political concerns: "You want to remember this . . . whoever ends up in control of China has won the Pacific war. . . . We'll defeat Japan, no question about that, it's just a matter of time . . . but China we need 'o worry about in the postwar period."[30]

What methods did Leahy employ in discharging his duties as the president's representative to the JCS? Although he became the primary channel for communications between Roosevelt and the Joint Chiefs, he religiously facilitated the military's unfettered access to the commander in chief. Instead of constituting a buffer between the president and the JCS, Leahy encouraged face-to-face dialogue. Throughout 1942 and 1943, the period when the framework of global strategy was being confirmed, Leahy and his colleagues met frequently with Roosevelt. Of comparable significance to this pattern of direct contact was an unobstructed flow of written communications. Reports and memoranda from the JCS were forwarded by Leahy to the president with minimal gloss or revision. As William H. McNeill noted in his landmark study of the Grand Alliance, "no other organ of the American or Anglo-American administration could so regularly secure Presidential attention to its proposals."[31]

Thomas Buell, King's biographer, has written, "given the frequent division between his JCS colleagues, Leahy's greatest contribution was to arbitrate behind closed doors by asking the right question."[32] It is difficult, however, to convey the precise nature of Leahy's interventions. The dry minutes of JCS meetings seldom capture the clash of personalities or the flavor of spirited debate. Fortunately, one veteran of the Joint Plans Staff, Admiral Robert Dennison, recorded his impressions of Leahy's technique.

> Leahy was the one that could bring this group together. He didn't really use any pressure, but his technique was most interesting. . . . Marshall, for example, would start discussing some plan of his, something he thought we ought to be doing next, and Leahy would say: "Well George, I'm just a simple sailor. Would you please back up and start from the beginning and make it simple, just tell me step one, two, and three, and so on."
>
> Well, Marshall or Arnold, or whoever . . . kept falling for this thing, and they would back up and explain it to this "simple old sailor." And as they did . . . they themselves would find out the weakness or misconception or that there was something wrong with it. So he didn't have to start out by saying: "This is a stupid idea and it won't work."[33]

Another hallmark of Leahy's style was his reluctance to meddle in the details of military plans and operations. With few exceptions, he communicated with American senior commanders through the formal channels established by the JCS.[34] Leahy also avoided intrusion into the internal affairs of the War and Navy Departments. Drawing upon his own experience as a chief of naval operations, he was inclined to respect the autonomy of the service chiefs in the administrative sphere.

One incident that illustrates Leahy's unwillingness to become entangled in the affairs of the military departments occurred in December 1944, when Navy Secretary James Forrestal requested Leahy's support in getting "new blood into the top Navy command." Leahy declined. "It was not part of my duty," he later explained. "As the President's chief of staff, it appeared best for me to remain as neutral as possible in matters of this nature."[35]

In 1951, when proposals for reorganization of the JCS were being floated, Admiral Richard Edwards, who had served as King's chief of staff, cited the model that Leahy had established for the role of chairman. Edwards wrote: "To do what has to be done there is a need for a man in a status comparable to that Admiral Leahy had during the war. . . . What we need, really, is a succession of Leahys, one for each generation."[36]

How do we place Leahy's wartime role in perspective? Perhaps the best way is to view him as a transitional figure in the evolution of the modern presidency.

On the eve of United States entry into World War II, political scientist Pendleton Herring, reflecting on the experience of the First World War, wrote that the president must be not only a "military coordinator" and "politician in chief" but also an "economic coordinator of industry and labor."[37] That Franklin Roosevelt succeeded in transcending the traditional role of the president as commander in chief to become the real *coordinator in chief* of American grand strategy in a global war was due—in no small measure—to the service rendered by William Leahy.

NOTES

1. Kent Roberts Greenfield, *American Strategy in World War II: A Reconsideration* (Baltimore: Johns Hopkins Univ. Press, 1963), 60. Greenfield was chief historian, Department of the Army, from 1946 to 1958.
2. Roosevelt to Amb. Joseph C. Grew, Jan. 21, 1941, U.S. Department of State, *Foreign Relations of the United States (FRUS), 1941*, vol. 7, *The Far East* (Washington, D.C.: GPO, 1956), 6.
3. Roosevelt fireside chat, Feb. 23, 1942, *Public Papers and Addresses of Franklin D. Roosevelt,* ed. Samuel I. Rosenman, 1942 ed. (New York: Random House, 1949), 105.
4. Roosevelt address to Congress, Sept. 17, 1943, *Public Papers and Addresses,* 1943 edition (New York: Random House, 1950), 388.

5. Leahy statement at 83rd meeting of CCS, May 13, 1943, U.S. Department of State, *FRUS*, 222. The text of Leahy's statement, which was written in the form of a memorandum for the CCS, was entitled "Global Strategy for the War."

6. For Leahy's early life and naval career, see Henry H. Adams, *Witness to Power: The Life of Fleet Admiral William D. Leahy* (Annapolis: Naval Institute Press, 1985); and John Major, "William Daniel Leahy," in *The Chiefs of Naval Operations,* ed. Robert William Love, Jr. (Annapolis: Naval Institute Press, 1980), 101-17.

7. Leahy's tenure as ambassador in Vichy is the subject of James H. Holmes, "Admiral Leahy in Vichy France, 1940-1942," (Ph.D. diss., George Washington University, 1974).

8. Editorial, *Times* (London), July 29, 1942, 5.

9. Editorial, *New York Herald-Tribune,* July 22, 1942.

10. *New York Herald-Tribune,* July 23, 1942, 1; Editorial, *Times* (London), July 23, 1942, 5.

11. Transcript of press conference, July 21, 1942, *Complete Presidential Press Conferences of Franklin D. Roosevelt,* vol. 20 (New York: Random House, 1972), 14; William D. Leahy, *I Was There* (New York: V. Gollancz, 1950), 97.

12. Walter Lippmann, "Today and Tomorrow," *Washington Post,* July 23, 1942.

13. Ibid.

14. Leahy, *I Was There,* 113. The issue was whether to authorize shipments of foodstuffs and other relief to French North Africa and occupied France. Roosevelt had instructed Leahy to tell the State Department and the Board of Economic Warfare (BEW) to resume shipments. BEW, headed by Vice President Henry A. Wallace, had balked. See minutes of BEW meeting, Sept. 7, 1942, BEW folder, Chairman's Files: Admiral Leahy, Records of the Joint Chiefs of Staff, RG 218, National Archives, Washington, D.C.

15. Leahy, *I Was There,* 96-97.

16. According to Marshall, Leahy seemed surprised when he was asked to preside at meetings of the Joint Chiefs. Larry I. Bland, Joellen K. Bland, and Sharon Ritenour Stevens, eds., *George C. Marshall: Interviews and Reminiscences for Forrest L. Pogue* (Lexington, Va.: G. C. Marshall Foundation, 1991), 432.

17. See diary entries for Nov. 4, Nov. 14, Nov. 16, Nov. 23, and Dec. 7, 1942, Papers of William D. Leahy, Library of Congress, Washington, D.C.

18. Roosevelt press conference, July 21, 1942.

19. Roosevelt to Leahy, July 27, 1942, Correspondence file, Papers of William D. Leahy, Operational Archives, Naval Historical Center, Washington, D.C. See also Leahy to Marvin H. McIntyre, Aug. 1, 1942, ibid.

20. See memorandum to Leahy, Sept. 4, 1942, enclosing draft telegram, Roosevelt to Churchill, Selected Correspondence file, Papers of George C. Marshall, George C. Marshall Library, Lexington, Virginia; telegram, Hopkins to Roosevelt, Sept. 22, 1942, and telegram, Hopkins to Roosevelt, Sept. 23, 1942, enclosing draft telegram, Roosevelt to Churchill, Map Room File,

box 15, Papers of Franklin D. Roosevelt, Franklin D. Roosevelt Library, Hyde Park, New York. In his telegram of September 22, Hopkins stated, "Will meet with Leahy this afternoon to send draft of reply for your consideration." In his message of September 23, Hopkins advised, "Admiral Leahy and I suggest that you reply to Prime Minister's No. 151 as follows."

21. Memorandum for Leahy, Sept. 23, 1942, Correspondence file, Leahy Papers, NHC.
22. Leahy, *I Was There,* 101. In 1947, Leahy provided a somewhat fuller description of his duties in a letter to Samuel I. Rosenman: "The President considered it necessary to the efficiency of our war effort to appoint his Chief of Staff a member of the Joint and Combined Chiefs in order that he might be assured of full daily information on the progress of the Allied war effort and have available means to exercise his constitutional authority on the strategical and tactical employment of the forces under his command." Leahy to Rosenman, June 19, 1947, Papers of William D. Leahy, State Historical Society of Wisconsin, Madison, Wisconsin.
23. Carl von Clausewitz, quoted in Peter Paret, "The Genius of *On War,*" in Clausewitz, *On War,* ed. and trans. Michael Howard and Peter Paret (Princeton: Princeton Univ. Press, 1976), 7.
24. Diary, April 3, 1943, Leahy Papers, LC; Leahy, *I Was There,* 1; and "United States Policy in World War II" folder, Leahy Papers, NHC.
25. Minutes of 34th meeting of the CCS, July 30, 1942, Records of the Joint Chiefs of Staff, RG 218, National Archives, Washington, D.C.
26. Ibid.
27. CCS 94, "Operations in 1942/43," July 24, 1942, RG 218, NA.
28. Minutes of the 34th meeting of the CCS, July 30, 1942; memorandum, Brig. Gen. W. B. Smith for the JCS, "Notes of a Conference held at the White House at 8:30 P.M., July 30, 1942," Aug. 1, 1942, Records of the War Department General Staff, RG 165, National Archives, Washington, D.C. In addition to Leahy and Brigadier General Smith, present at the meeting with Roosevelt were General Henry H. Arnold and Captain John L. McCrea, the president's naval aide.
29. Leahy, *I Was There,* 108; Minutes of 83rd meeting of the CCS, May 13, 1943, *FRUS: Washington and Quebec,* 44.
30. Transcript of oral history interview with Adm. Richard L. Conolly, United States Naval Institute, Annapolis, Maryland.
31. William H. McNeill, *America, Britain, and Russia: Their Cooperation and Conflict* (London: Oxford Univ. Press, 1953), 109n.
32. Thomas B. Buell, *Master of Sea Power: A Biography of Fleet Admiral Ernest J. King* (Boston: Little, Brown Co., 1980), 312.
33. Transcript of oral history interview with Adm. Robert L. Dennison, United States Naval Institute, Annapolis, Maryland.
34. One exception to this pattern was Leahy's occasional correspondence with MacArthur. See, for example, MacArthur to Leahy, Aug. 7, 1944, Leahy Papers, SHSW.

35. Diary, Dec. 24, 1944, Leahy Papers, LC; Leahy, *I Was There*, 283.
36. R. S. Edwards to Ernest J. King, Mar. 27, 1951, Papers of Ernest J. King, box 17, Library of Congress, Washington, D.C.
37. Pendleton Herring, *The Impact of War* (New York: Farrar & Rinehart, 1941), 159-61.

TEN

ROOSEVELT AND STRATEGY IN THE PACIFIC

Thomas B. Buell

WHEN ED MAROLDA FIRST ASKED ME to undertake this chapter my initial reaction was that Roosevelt had exerted no more than a nominal influence on the strategy in the Pacific. My way of thinking had always been that Fleet Admiral King specifically, and the Joint Chiefs of Staff generally, were the architects of strategy in the Pacific. Its members, after considerable discussion, if not strife, came to common agreement among themselves, and then got the British chiefs of staff to concur, again, after coercion and prolonged and heated debate. As I am not a Roosevelt scholar per se, but rather a naval historian and biographer who has tended to look at Roosevelt as King saw him, I was accustomed to regarding Roosevelt's role primarily as confirming what the military chiefs had already decided to do.

But in researching this chapter, I came to realize that Roosevelt did indeed influence the Pacific strategy, both directly and indirectly, as well as consciously and unconsciously. To begin with, Roosevelt certainly influenced strategy in the Pacific by the people he chose to run the Navy. He obviously wanted people who thought offensively and aggressively, a criteria that had radically changed from his prewar practices. It will be recalled that in peacetime, Roosevelt had selected chiefs of naval operations (CNOs) with whom he felt comfortable, whom he knew personally, and who had the patience and diplomacy needed to work with Congress. This is why he picked the tactful Harold R. Stark to follow William D. Leahy as CNO in 1939. Irascible, outspoken Ernest J. King, never a member of Roosevelt's inner circle, had not been seriously considered. Everyone thought that King's career was over when King, despite his brilliance and his singular professional qualifications, was passed over in favor of Stark.

But King had important advocates in Secretary of the Navy Frank Knox and Admiral Stark, for they knew how much the Navy needed King's toughness and leadership. Hence King had stayed alive, had taken over the Atlantic Fleet, and had been promoted to admiral of full rank while fighting U-boats in an undeclared war in the Atlantic. He made many trips from his flagship in Newport to the Navy Department to confer with Secretary of the Navy Knox, who came to respect King's abilities. Thus, on the recommendation of Knox, shortly after Pearl Harbor, Roosevelt appointed King as Commander in Chief, U.S. Fleet, and later gave him a second hat as CNO when Stark became redundant. Thus, by this decision on the part of the president, King was placed in the position where he could drive the strategy for the war in the Pacific. Roosevelt similarly affected Pacific strategy by appointing Admiral Chester W. Nimitz as Commander in Chief, Pacific Ocean Areas, and of course, General Douglas MacArthur as Commander in Chief, Southwest Pacific Area. While Roosevelt might not have known, at the time he appointed these three men, what strategies they would advocate, he was reasonably certain they would be aggressive, steady, smart, and driven by a fighting spirit.

King was still trying to find his office furniture when Churchill and his service chiefs came to Washington in late December 1941, shortly after Pearl Harbor, to deliberate war strategy, now that the

United States and Great Britain were active allies. Looming large was the Germany First doctrine, which Churchill wanted to reinforce, as he knew that the Americans would want to retaliate against the Japanese. There had been little opportunity for King to see Roosevelt beforehand, so the president and his new naval chief were largely strangers to each other. Now King, for the first time, could calibrate the president during the impromptu and largely unstructured meetings with the British. King knew how difficult it was to fathom what Roosevelt was thinking in terms of military commitments, for when King had been Commander in Chief, U.S. Atlantic Fleet (CINCLANT) during the past year, Stark had told him of the frustration of trying to get Roosevelt to enunciate a consistent policy for the employment of the fleet.[1]

King now saw a decisive Roosevelt, who soon made it clear that he wanted his Navy to strike back at the Japanese. Furthermore, the president rebuked the Navy—in the very presence of the British—for the succession of disasters in the Pacific, particularly the withdrawal of the Wake Island relief force. Secretary Knox let it be known he could not understand why Vice Admiral William Pye had turned it back. In a conversation with Churchill, Knox asked, "What would you do with your admiral in a case like this?" Replied Churchill, "It is dangerous to meddle with admirals when they say they can't do things. They have always got the weather or fuel or something to argue about."[2]

Such attitudes from *his* admirals were intolerable to Roosevelt. He wanted action. A force of cruisers and destroyers, he said, could seek out smaller Japanese forces and do battle, and, if they came in contact with a superior force, could withdraw at high speed. The sinking of HMS *Repulse* and HMS *Prince of Wales* off Singapore apparently had not taught Roosevelt that warships could not outrun aircraft. And yet, while Roosevelt's tactical ideas were wholly impractical, his resolve to hit back at the Japanese was beyond question. This resolution was Roosevelt's greatest contribution to the development of naval strategy in the Pacific.

King's strategic vision was first expressed when he formally became Commander in Chief, U.S. Fleet (COMINCH) on December 31, 1941. It probably was not until then that Roosevelt found out King's intentions, for the admiral sent a directive to Admiral Nimitz that was the foundation for naval strategy during the early part of the war. The first priority, said King, was to safeguard the sea lines of communication from the United States to Hawaii and thence to Midway. The second priority was to maintain communications with Australia, chiefly by safeguarding the Hawaii-Samoa line of communication.[3] Whether King cleared this beforehand with Roosevelt is unknown, but my guess is that he did not, as Roosevelt was fully engaged in dealing with his house guest, Winston Churchill.

Having set the early stage, let us now examine in more detail how Roosevelt influenced naval strategy throughout the war. Here is one example of what I term his indirect or unconscious influence: King and the Army chief of staff, General George C. Marshall, had prolonged disagreements on American and Allied strategy, but rarely, if ever, did they ask Roosevelt to choose between them. The reason, I believe, was that they thought it was very possible that Roosevelt would decide upon something that would satisfy neither the Navy nor the Army. Thus they were motivated to work out their problems, and then come before Roosevelt with a united front. As a corollary to this, both King and Marshall strove to get Roosevelt to buy in with the Joint Chiefs of Staff (JCS) point of view, because they were concerned that Roosevelt was given to compromise in his dealings with Churchill and might defer to British demands.

Having said this, are there instances when Roosevelt did have a direct, positive, beneficial influence on Pacific strategy? The answer is certainly "yes." Consider the employment of the British fleet in the last months of the Pacific war. Churchill wanted to do it primarily for political reasons, to show that Great Britain had contributed to victory in the Pacific, had redeemed its reputation after its anemic performance in Southeast Asia and the Far East, and that Great

Britain had claim to the retention of its eastern prewar empire, primarily India but also Singapore, Burma, and Hong Kong.

King—and the Navy in general—opposed Churchill's scheme, not for political ideology but for logistical reasons. The Royal Navy was considered a liability because of its "short legs," as it was without mobile logistical support so vital for operations in the Pacific, and King had no intention of supporting British warships with American resources. King and his admirals also perhaps wanted full credit for winning the war against Japan. Knowing the intensity of King's opposition, Churchill put his offer directly to Roosevelt in front of the JCS. Roosevelt didn't blink; he accepted immediately, overruling King. It was the right decision, as the Royal Navy was an invaluable reinforcement and ally in the summer of 1945 when the American navy was taking such a battering from the Japanese kamikazes. Admiral Raymond A. Spruance, for one, was everlastingly grateful that the British were there to help him. I doubt that Roosevelt had the kamikazes in mind when he said he would welcome the Royal Navy, and his decision was made for reasons on which we can only speculate, but nonetheless it was a decision that profoundly influenced the strategy of the war.

But how did Roosevelt influence strategy on a day-by-day basis? Roosevelt considered himself an expert in two areas of naval strategy. One was his natural interest in naval matters that covered decades. As president before the war he had been essentially his own secretary of the Navy. The other was his knowledge of the geography of the Pacific, because he was a stamp collector and owned a portfolio of National Geographic maps. Once, early in the war, he invited Secretary of War Henry L. Stimson to spend an evening with him. Stimson was an advocate of Germany First, and he therefore opposed any large-scale American commitment in the Pacific. Roosevelt felt that Stimson was perhaps too narrow minded and had to be educated on the elements of Pacific naval strategy. So, with maps spread over a table, the president lectured his secretary of war on the inter relationship between geography and the employment of naval forces in a war in the Pacific.[4]

Roosevelt and King met privately time and again, often for long periods, and what they said to each other is largely unrecorded. I have to believe that those conversations were two way, that King respected Roosevelt's judgment and incorporated some of Roosevelt's ideas into his own, and vice versa. One example might have been China. Roosevelt and King saw alike the need to keep China in the war, but for somewhat different reasons. Roosevelt acted on the longstanding policy of protecting China's sovereignty, while King regarded China as a source of manpower to tie down the bulk of the Japanese army, and as a base for the eventual blockade of Japan. The impact on strategy in this instance was complementary.

Whatever passed between them in private, King did say that Roosevelt trusted King's judgment and was grateful for King's candor and straightforward way of expressing himself. More to the point, Roosevelt ultimately supported the strategy that King took before his colleagues in the Combined Chiefs of Staff. In meetings with the British, he and the president would exchange glances, and King with no more than a nod of the head would advise the president on the issue on the table.[5]

When King turned age 64 in November 1942, the mandatory retirement age, he worried whether Roosevelt would allow him to continue on active duty. He sent a letter to the president. "It appears proper that I should bring to your notice the fact that the record shows that I shall attain the age of 64 years on November 23rd next—one month from today. I am, as always, at your service." The letter was returned with a note from Roosevelt scrawled on the bottom: "E.J.K. So what, old top? I may send you a Birthday present! FDR." That simple note reassured King that Roosevelt wanted him for the long run, and King was elated.[6]

There was a special relationship of absolute trust between the president and the JCS. They served at his pleasure and were responsible solely to him. It is an interesting fact that Roosevelt refused to ask Congress to give the JCS legal standing because he wanted them to have the widest possible latitude in directing the war. This bothered the chiefs to a great extent, because they wanted official recognition of their existence and a sense of permanence. But Roosevelt did not want restraints placed on the scope of their authority, nor did he want congressional hearings on the conduct of the war which would have been inevitable had he submitted legislation for congressional approval. All that, believed the president, could wait until after the war, which is indeed what happened.

The only person to leave the JCS during the war was Stark, because he was redundant, and the only person to come aboard after the war began was Leahy. King, Marshall, and Arnold were there from start to finish. The way they did business with the president was entirely different than the British way with Churchill and his chiefs of staff. The British met with the prime minister almost daily, and it was an ordeal for the men in uniform. I've often wondered how they found time to work, much less sleep. In contrast, meetings between Roosevelt and the JCS were infrequent, and he essentially let them do their jobs. Yet King also knew that Roosevelt would not rubber-stamp what King wanted to do. King had to convince Roosevelt with logic and sound reasoning.

The most publicized instance of Roosevelt's involvement with strategy in the Pacific was his famous cruise to Hawaii in the summer of 1944 to confer with MacArthur and Nimitz. It was an election year, and in King's view the president was playing the role of commander in chief for the benefit of public consumption. Yet Roosevelt knew at the time that the JCS were split on the next step in the Pacific. The campaign in the Marianas had begun and MacArthur had rolled up New Guinea, but there was no consensus as to what was next. King wanted to seize Formosa, even though his Pacific commanders opposed it, while Marshall and MacArthur naturally wanted to assault the Philippines. Thus, with the JCS at an impasse, it was not out of order for Roosevelt to hear directly from his on-the-scene commanders to try to get the JCS to come to an agreement. So, in effect, Roosevelt was interested both in getting the JCS off dead center and in helping his reelection.

The upshot of Roosevelt's Hawaii meeting was that he supported the invasion of the Philippines but did not rule out Formosa. As a consequence, King agreed to the Philippines, but Marshall would not agree to Formosa as a quid pro quo. It would take months of wrangling within the JCS before King finally dropped Formosa and agreed to Iwo Jima and Okinawa, as recommended by Nimitz and Spruance. Hence Roosevelt had nudged the JCS along in their Pacific strategy, but his meeting in Hawaii was but one element in the overall sequence of events that led to the ultimate decisions and commitments.

King also recognized that Roosevelt—from decades of custom and personal preference—wanted to keep his hand in the daily affairs of the Navy Department, both with respect to administration and to operations, but King kept him at arm's length to the extent possible. "The admirals are really something to cope with, and I should know," Roosevelt once told a colleague. "To change anything in the Na-a-vy is like punching a feather bed. You punch it with your right and you punch it with your left until you are finally exhausted, and then you find the damn bed just as it was before you started punching."[7]

Roosevelt won a few and lost a few in his tussles with King. Very early in the war King tried to reorganize the Navy Department to make the bureau chiefs responsible to him, not the secretary of the Navy. He failed to clear this with the president, and, when Roosevelt found out, he made King rescind the order. Normally, King tried to coordinate with the president. He did this in large measure through the president's naval aide—King told the aide to tell the president everything the Navy Department was doing, and to hold nothing back. The aide later told King and his admirals that should they ever do anything they wanted to conceal from Roosevelt, they were not to tell the aide about it. In any event, I think the aides—senior captains handpicked by King—were an important conduit for information and coordination between the president and the admiral.

As to operations, early in the war Roosevelt sent an operational order directly to Admiral Thomas C. Hart as to how to employ his ships in the western Pacific. King naturally objected to what he considered unwarranted interference, and he took measures to ensure that the president never again did this. Roosevelt did keep abreast of operational developments in the White House War Room, which was patterned after the British model.

Thus Roosevelt was kept well informed, he knew what the strategy was in the Pacific, and I am sure that it was a joint product of the thinking of both Roosevelt and King. This was most apparent in 1942, when King had 32 recorded meetings in the White House with Roosevelt, and probably many more that were unrecorded. Afterward the recorded meetings declined in number; 8 in 1943, 9 in 1944, and 1 in 1945. There are two probable reasons why the numbers declined. One was that the Pacific strategy was fairly well established by May of 1943 as a consequence of the Trident Conference, and meetings were no longer as necessary. I think another reason was that, when Leahy became chief of staff to the president in July 1942, he became an important conduit of information between the JCS and the president. King very likely was content to let his fellow admiral deal with the president on routine matters. In any event, Roosevelt progressively allowed King a free hand to run the Navy, the Pacific strategy was in place, and so the need for King to see Roosevelt no longer was urgent.

How, then, shall we summarize Roosevelt's influence on strategy in the Pacific? It was primarily through his statements of policy, his leadership, and his fighting spirit. He gave moral support to King and the Navy to pursue an aggressive strategy against Japan, so that the United States Army and Great Britain had to acquiesce to sending resources to the Pacific despite the Germany First doctrine. He mobilized the nation's war production capability so that there were enough ships, planes, weapons, and manpower to fight simultaneously in Europe and on two fronts in the Pacific. He picked the right men to develop the strategy for the Pacific, he supported them in every possible way, and he gave them some ideas of his own, although to what extent we may never know. Roosevelt was a magnificent wartime president, whom I rank with Abraham Lincoln. They were the giants and the saviors of our country in the times of America's greatest test of national survival.

NOTES

1. Thomas B. Buell, *Master of Sea Power: A Biography of Fleet Admiral Ernest J. King* (Boston: Little Brown and Co., 1980), 151-80.
2. Ibid., 167.
3. Ibid., 167-69.
4. Ibid., 242.
5. Ibid., 240-52.
6. Ibid., 187.
7. Quoted in James M. Burns, *Roosevelt: The Soldier of Freedom* (New York: Harcourt Brace Jovanovich, 1970), 352.

ELEVEN

ROOSEVELT AND KING: THE WAR IN THE ATLANTIC AND EUROPEAN THEATERS[1]

Jeffrey G. Barlow

GIVEN HIS EARLIER BACKGROUND as assistant secretary of the Navy during World War I and his close association with Navy leaders during his first two terms as president, one cannot doubt Franklin Delano Roosevelt's special affection for the U.S. Navy. Nonetheless, once the United States entered World War II in December 1941, FDR found himself thrust into an unaccustomed role as the country's wartime commander in chief, and the air of easygoing familiarity common to his prewar dealings with the Navy quickly vanished forever. Indeed, referring to the U.S. Army's regular complaint during the war that he was partial toward the Navy, the president remarked to Budget Director Harold D. Smith in August 1943 that "he had had more trouble with the Navy in this war than with the Army."[2]

Roosevelt and King

To understand the wartime relationship between Franklin Roosevelt and Ernest King, it is necessary first to know something about their personalities and outlooks. FDR both as a man and as President of the United States possessed an interesting complexity of personality traits.[3] By nature an optimist with a zest for life, he always tried to appear buoyant and self-confident, even in his last years, when fatigue and ill health increasingly marked his features. Roosevelt was a charming man in person. Yet, he was often insensitive to his wife's feelings and emotionally distant with his immediate family. As James MacGregor Burns commented, "No one—not even his wife or sons—felt that he could get close enough to the President to understand him."[4]

"A gregarious man who preferred talking to reading or writing," Franklin Roosevelt's manner of addressing issues in the Oval Office was to talk about them.[5] Nonetheless, the more serious the issue at hand (and the more undecided he was in his own mind about how to deal with it), the more likely FDR was to avoid it altogether; preferring instead to weave a conversational tapestry of his own stories and reminiscences that allowed his visitors little chance to interject their views. George C. Marshall, his wartime Army chief of staff, recalled, ". . . I was always involved in the problem of finding an opportunity to state my case. . . . When I would have something particularly disagreeable—something that was very difficult for him to do at that time—and he didn't want such a matter to be brought up, he would be very communicative and would talk continually, and I would never get a look-in until the time had expired."[6]

Franklin Roosevelt was also a president who liked to keep his options open, never making a decision "before its time" if he could help it. One of the ways he accomplished this feat was by leaving his visitors with the impression that he agreed with their views. As Mrs. Roosevelt told Forrest Pogue when he interviewed her, "I am afraid that my husband had a habit of letting people leave his office thinking that he had agreed with them."[7] Another method he frequently employed was keeping his advisers in the dark about his moves. His relations with the senior military officers who made up the wartime Joint Chiefs of Staff was no different.[8] As General Marshall remarked:

> . . . Mr. Roosevelt was always very sensitive about the reports on his own conduct of affairs. He didn't want a record of cabinet meetings. He didn't give us the messages he was sending half the time. He would communicate with Churchill . . . and I would be wholly unaware of it, though it directly affected the affairs of the army and the air and maybe the navy.
>
> In this peculiar way I kept track of this matter. When a message would go from the president to Churchill . . . that would immediately go in the special distribution that was regulated by the affairs of the British officialdom so that everybody that should know that immediately got a copy of it. . . . [When Field Marshal Sir John Dill, who represented the British Chiefs of Staff in Washington, received his copy, he] would come over to my office, and I would get Mr. Roosevelt's message through . . . Dill. Otherwise, I wouldn't know what it was. I had to be very careful that nobody knew this—no one in the War Department—and certainly not the [British] chiefs of staff, because Dill would be destroyed in a minute if this was discovered. But he knew I had to have it . . . and he just brought it to me and read it to me. . . .
>
> . . . Why should the British chiefs of staff have it—it was from our president—and the American chiefs of staff not have it? But it was just Mr. Roosevelt's desire for secrecy.[9]

While there is no gainsaying his special affection for the Navy, it must be kept in mind that FDR's affection was tempered by his political pragmatism. It should be remembered, for example, that his support for rebuilding the U.S. Navy's strength during his first two terms as president was restrained not only by his desire to avoid excessive spending for naval construction during the Great Depression but also by his wish to keep the United States from becoming the first of the major signatory powers of the Washington and London Naval Treaties to move away from its naval arms limitation principles.[10] In fact, during the mid-1930s, Roosevelt went to great lengths to put off allowing the Navy to arm its new battleships with 16-inch guns, despite the overwhelming evidence of his naval advisers that such a step was vital for maintaining their offensive capabilities against the battleships of potential enemies. Admiral Harold R. "Betty" Stark, chief of naval operations at the outbreak of World War II, recalled in a 1944 letter to Secretary of the Navy Frank Knox:

> This all occurred when I was Chief of the Bureau of Ordnance back in 1934. . . . I was nearly a year arguing this question out frequently with the President, who finally let me have my 16" guns. I say "finally" because I carried the ships on both a 14" and a 16" design up to a point where [the] final choice had to made to continue their building, and then the President okay'd the 16", and for which I have always been very grateful, and so has the Navy, and incidently, so is Winston Churchill, who says that his only regret was that theirs were not so powerful.[11]

Furthermore, it must be acknowledged that as a former senior civilian member of the Navy Department, FDR viewed the Navy's admirals with an amused but jaundiced eye and remained ever watchful lest flag officers attempt to expand their influence over areas he viewed as the rightful preserve of the service's civilian secretariat. With U.S. entry into the war less than a year away, he began a December 1940 memo to Frank Knox, turning down the secretary's request for a large increase in the strength of the Navy's enlisted personnel, thusly:

Dear Frank:—

The dear, delightful officers of the regular Navy are doing to you today just what others [sic] officers were trying to do to me a quarter of a century ago. If you and I were regular officers of the Navy, you and I would do the same thing![12]

Where Franklin Roosevelt was a genial conversationalist and a convivial spirit, the Navy's senior admiral from March 1942 onward, Ernest J. King, was anything but that. Indeed, shortly after King had taken over as Commander in Chief, United States Fleet (COMINCH) in December 1941, a rumor was going around that he had commented of himself, "When they get into trouble, they send for the son-of-bitches." Captain John McCrea, President Roosevelt's naval aide, had had the temerity to ask Admiral King if this was true, saying, "I hear you made the statement that when the going gets rough they send for the S.O.B.s." King quickly replied, "No, I didn't think of it—but would have *if* I had."[13]

Historian Robert Love has characterized Ernie King as "suspicious, cruel, vain, rude, and irascible—and yet the most brilliant naval leader of the era," noting as well, that, "[o]n the job, he seemed always to be angry or annoyed."[14] The admiral's biographer, Thomas Buell, highlighted another aspect of King's demeanor when, in writing of his time as commanding officer of the carrier *Lexington,* he remarked, "Praise was given grudgingly and then only in private. Censure was swift, devastating and before a cloud of witnesses."[15] Admiral Francis S. "Frog" Low, who served closely with Admiral King during the war, perhaps provided a fragmentary view into the reasons for King's irascible personality when he remarked in an unpublished memoir that King had told him that, as a new ensign, "he early realized that he had a tendency to be 'soft' and that he knew, if he was to progress in the Navy, he would have to get a grip on himself."[16]

Whatever the reason for his personality, Ernie King as an admiral was a fire breather. Where FDR was given to pleasant obfuscation in the face of issues he preferred not to deal with, King was direct, abrupt, tactless, and undiplomatic by turns, but, above all, he was decisive. He respected Franklin Roosevelt as the president and was fully aware that his authority as COMINCH/ CNO depended solely on Roosevelt's continued support, but he had no special love for FDR the man, commenting several years after the president's death that Roosevelt was a "tricky" man who "liked to pull things."[17]

For his part, FDR looked on King with bemused affection. The admiral was a "doer"—to Roosevelt, one of those rare officers who could drive the often-sluggish Navy bureaucracy into producing war-winning results through the force of his will. The president's wry appreciation of King was noticeable in a January 1943 conversation he had with his son Elliott on his voyage across the Atlantic for the Casablanca Conference, when he humorously remarked, "You know, Elliott, we have a tough enough time convincing Admiral King that any shipping or landing-craft should be diverted to the Atlantic theaters—only the scene of the main war. Can you imagine how he felt when Burma was mentioned? He's a grand Navy man. 'Wars can only be won by sea power; furthermore, only the Pacific theater is a naval theater; therefore, the Pacific theater must be the most important.'"[18]

Nonetheless, unlike his immediate predecessors as chief of naval operations, Admiral William D. Leahy and Admiral Harold Stark, King was neither a Roosevelt acquaintance of long standing nor a personal friend, and he kept it that way for the duration. Like his Army counterpart, George Marshall, King refused to become too friendly with the president. As Marshall later explained his own reasoning behind this decision, "It's very difficult if you've been at a dinner the night before a meeting and have told stories together and have been very happy, patting each other on the back, to go into a meeting the next day and say, 'Sir, that's not something I think we should do.'"[19]

FDR apparently made one attempt to convert his relationship with Admiral King into the kind of easygoing, written bantering he had had on occasion with "Betty" Stark. In August 1942, he wrote King:

> Dear Ernie:
>
> You will remember "the sweet young thing" whom I told about Douglas MacArthur rowing his family from Corregidor to Australia —and later told about Shangri-La as the take-off place for the Tokio [sic] bombers.
>
> Well, she came in to dinner last night and this time *she* told *me* something.
>
> She said "We are going to win this war. The Navy is tough. And the toughest man in the Navy—Admiral King—proves it. He shaves every morning with a blowtorch."
>
> Glad to know you!
>
> P.S. I am trying to verify another rumor—that you cut your toenails with a torpedo net cutter.[20]

Ernie King, who was probably not amused, did not rise to the bait, and his rather formal relationship with the president continued as before.

Turning from Roosevelt and King's personal relationship to their professional association during the war, there are a number of issues relating to the war in the Atlantic and Mediterranean theaters that are worthy of some discussion. For reasons of brevity, only two will be examined here—the Battle of the Atlantic and the decision to carry out Operation Torch.

The Battle of the Atlantic

On December 7, 1941, the United States found itself unexpectedly plunged into a war with Japan. Four days later, following Hitler's declaration of war against the United States, the U.S. Navy was at war in both the Atlantic and the Pacific Oceans with a fleet that was still months away from being a "Two-Ocean Navy."

In January 1942, the first small group of German Type IX-C U-boats began operating off the eastern coast of the United States and began sinking increasing numbers of unescorted U.S. merchant ships, in what soon became known as the U-boats' "Second Happy Time." As more German submarines arrived on station, U-boat sinkings in the Atlantic during the first half of 1942—the largest portion being from areas off the east and southeast coasts of the United States—rose from some 296,000 tons in January to a new high score of 652,000 tons in June before slacking off gradually during the last half of the year.[21]

By late February 1942, as U.S. merchant ship sinkings mounted, an alarmed Franklin Roosevelt issued an executive order directing Navy Secretary Frank Knox to "protect vessels, harbors, ports and waterfront facilities." The president informed Knox that Admiral King's decision to put Rear Admiral Adolphus Andrews in complete charge of the Atlantic coastal patrol, as commander of the Eastern Sea Frontier, was good "but it has taken a hell of a long time to get it done." And he further suggested to the Navy secretary that the U.S. Coast Guard, which knew "infinitely more" about coastal patrolling and harbor protection than the Navy did, should be "put in charge of this work on the whole of the East coast."[22] Knox quickly reported to the president that he had placed the Coast Guard in charge of protecting shipping in port and waterfront property, but he carefully sidestepped the larger (and more dangerous) implications posed by Roosevelt's comments. A few months later, in speaking about the latest stage of the Battle of the Atlantic in an interview with Samuel Eliot Morison, the Navy's newly appointed historian of wartime naval operations, FDR admitted that "the Navy has muffed it." Morison noted the president's comment that the "trouble with U.S. naval officers is [that they] can't think in terms of ships of less than 1000 tons. . . . [They] haven't now,

[and] won't have until August sufficient patrol boats to handle it themselves."[23]

In point of fact, there were many factors behind the U.S. Navy's poor showing in the Battle of the Atlantic during the first months of the war, and some of them, although FDR might not have wanted to admit it, were due to decisions he had made. As just one example, in September 1940, President Roosevelt signed the destroyer-bases agreement that had been negotiated with Prime Minister Churchill, which transferred to Britain 50 World War I– vintage, four-stack American destroyers (plus 5 Navy PBY long-range patrol planes and 5 Army B-17 Flying Fortresses) in exchange for 99-year leases of bases in British possessions in Newfoundland, Bermuda, the Bahamas, Jamaica, St. Lucia, Trinidad, and British Guiana.[24] Yet, as FDR clearly realized, those 50 destroyers constituted a significant portion of the U.S. Navy's reserve escort forces, which would be needed if the United States entered the war. In fact, other destroyers of a similar vintage had been recommissioned for escort duties during the Neutrality Patrol in 1939.[25] Thus, when the United States did come into the war in December 1941, the Navy found itself with few readily available ships to reinforce the woefully inadequate number of escorts based in the Atlantic.[26]

From the outset of the German submarine attacks on the U.S. East Coast, there were calls from many quarters for the institution of coastal convoying. This was all well and good, but the few destroyers available in the Atlantic were already busily convoying American transatlantic troop shipping, which, at the American-British Arcadia Conference in the latter part of December 1941, had been determined to have the first call on American naval resources in the Atlantic.[27] Moreover, Admiral King, who had a thorough understanding of the importance of convoying in ultimately defeating the U-boat attacks, believed that "inadequately escorted convoys were worse than none" and refused to allow coastal convoying until the available escort forces could be beefed up. His point of view on this matter was strongly conveyed to Under Secretary of War Robert P. Patterson in early March 1942 by Under Secretary of the Navy James V. Forrestal, who stressed: "A plan for coastal convoys is under consideration but at present the forces available are inadequate to provide proper escort. It is inadvisable to form vessels into large convoys until effective protection can be furnished, since this would give enemy submarines the opportunity to attack large formations instead of single ships with consequent increase rather than decrease in losses."[28]

Throughout the first months of the war, FDR continued to use his "bully pulpit" to hector Navy leaders on the issue of how to defeat the U-boat attacks. Employing small boats for patrolling was one of his continuing pet projects.[29] In June 1942, FDR wrote a letter to Rear Admiral Andrews, Eastern Sea Frontier commander, in which he spelled out his conception for using these small craft. He wrote:

> It is the tendency of the Navy to seek perfection. The Navy is not a good hand at improvising. That is a just criticism with which I know you agree. When a small vessel—40, 50 or 60 feet in length is taken over there are two rules that should be observed:
> (a) Use the men who are familiar with the individual ship. . . . They may be too old for Navy physicals. They may limp when they walk. They may have to wear glasses. . . . But the point is that they know their own vessel and they can be supplemented by a radio man and one man aft to "cut the string" and let a depth charge roll over the stern. . . .
> (b) Incidentally, all that most of these little vessels need is a machine gun forward, a radio telephone and three or four depth charges aft. . . .
> The whole purpose is to keep the submarine down both day and night. . . .[30]

Ernie King's verbal response to this daring scheme is mercifully lost to us. Nonetheless, King did go along with the president's idea of converting nearly 4,000 privately owned pleasure craft for antisubmarine warfare (ASW), despite his obvious misgivings.[31]

In a similar fashion, King went along with the Churchill-inspired scheme, forced on him by Roosevelt, to outfit Q-ships—antisubmarine ships disguised as unarmed merchantmen. But then, as Richard Parmenter, the former skipper of one of these Q-ships—*Irene Forsyte*—observed after the war, "I note that on March 14, 1942, my diary records seven ships sunk in seventy hours. This, I believe, was an important factor in the determination of Cominch in turning to any means however desperate."[32]

Despite his obvious desire for an early solution to the U-boat problem, it is important to note that Franklin Roosevelt was careful not to meddle in the operational decisions of his admirals. Fortunately, he let Frank Knox and Ernie King work through the myriad problems posed for the Navy Department by the war. In this vital regard, he clearly differed from his British counterpart, Winston Churchill. The prime minister, who considered himself something of a professional strategist, was not averse during the war to making operational decisions that were completely contrary to the carefully considered advice of his military staff. These unfortunate officers, in the words of U.S. Army Major General Ray Barker, were subjected all too frequently to the effects of the "Prime Minister's sun-lamp."[33]

Gradually, the Battle of the Atlantic began moving in the Allies' favor. In April 1942, King instituted a limited, daylight convoy system from New York south to Key West, and in June he put into place a full-fledged, round-the-clock Interlocking Convoy System running from Halifax, Nova Scotia, to Key West, forcing the U-boats into the Caribbean in search of easier targets. During the course of the next few months, the Caribbean and the Gulf of Mexico also came under convoy protection, and the U-boats moved back into the North Atlantic in their quest for easier pickings.[34] Within another year, new ASW weapons and vastly increased numbers of Allied ships and aircraft had broken the back of the German U-boat threat in the Atlantic, and although the German commander, Admiral Doenitz, later attempted to reassert primacy against Allied convoys in that ocean, his U-boats were unable to gain the upper hand during the final years of the war.

Operation Torch

Torch, the plan to launch an Allied invasion of French North Africa, was one of those few instances during World War II when Franklin Roosevelt formally overruled his Joint Chiefs of Staff. As far as the war against Germany was concerned, FDR, during the summer and fall of 1942, was clearly still under the strategic sway of Winston Churchill. In the spring of that year, the American chiefs, principally Marshall and King, had put forward two plans for a cross-Channel invasion of German-held France—Operation Bolero, a full-scale invasion by some 48 divisions, scheduled for April 1, 1943, and Operation Sledgehammer, a contingency landing on the northern coast of France in 1942 by a much smaller number of divisions, in the event of an emergency such as the pending defeat of the Soviet Union by German forces.[35]

The British, however, were never very fond of either of these plans. In a message to the president dated June 20, 1942, the British prime minister wrote, "But in case no plan can be made in which any responsible authority has good confidence, and consequently no engagement on a substantial scale in France is possible in September 1942, what else are we going to do? Can we afford to stand idle in the Atlantic Theatre during the whole of 1942?" Churchill went on to suggest that, in this setting, Operation Gymnast—an earlier plan for an invasion of North Africa—should be studied.[36]

Less than three weeks later, Churchill made it evident to Roosevelt that he and his Chiefs of Staff found Sledgehammer totally impractical; telling the president on July 8:

1. No responsible British General, Admiral or Air Marshal is prepared to recommend SLEDGEHAMMER as a practicable operation in 1942. . . .

2. . . . But far more serious is the fact that according to Mountbatten [Chief of Combined Operations] if we interrupt the training of the troops we should apart from the loss of landing craft etc delay ROUNDUP or 1943 BOLERO for at least two or three months. . . .

. . .

4. I am sure GYMNAST is by far the best chance for effective relief to the Russian front in 1942.[37]

The reaction of the Joint Chiefs of Staff to this decisive rejection of their plans for European operations was electric. Marshall quickly drafted a "Memorandum For The President," which stated:

The [British] proposal means no BOLERO in 1942 and an inadequate and probably ineffective BOLERO, if any, in the spring of 1943.

It is also our opinion that under existing circumstances the effect of GYMNAST would be indecisive. Therefore, if we undertake the GYMNAST operation at the expense of BOLERO we would nowhere be pressing decisively against the enemy.

If the British attitude as to BOLERO must be accepted, it is our opinion that we should turn to the Pacific, and, using all existing and available dispositions and installations, strike decisively against Japan.[38]

Admiral King promptly signed Marshall's memorandum, remarking later that he had supported the proposal "in order to put pressure on the British."[39]

George Marshall commented after the war that his proposal to shift the full U.S. effort had been a bluff. But bluff or not, FDR quickly called it. On July 12, Roosevelt telephoned from Hyde Park and directed the Joint Chiefs of Staff to send him "this afternoon by plane a detailed comprehensive outline of the plans [for the shift to the Pacific], including estimated time and over-all totals of ships, planes, and ground forces."[40] In a "Memorandum For The President" drafted by the Navy and signed by the Joint Chiefs of Staff that same day, King, Marshall, and Army Air Forces chief Henry H. Arnold were forced to admit, "There is no completed detailed plan for major offensive operations in the Pacific."[41] Two days later, FDR sent word to Marshall that he did not approve the Pacific alternative, that he wanted to meet with the chiefs the next day, and that he wanted Marshall, King, and Harry Hopkins to leave for London as soon as possible to work out a plan for operations in 1942 with their British counterparts.[42]

Once in London and faced with continued British intransigence on the issue of operations against northern Europe in 1942, Marshall and King were forced to compromise. As George Marshall recalled:

> King and I went over in July and quickly found out that we couldn't get anywhere on either of the plans. . . .
> . . . One morning before breakfast, I sat down at Claridge's in my room and began to write. I recognized we couldn't do SLEDGE-HAMMER and that there was no immediate prospect of ROUNDUP [the revised Bolero].
> What was the least harmful diversion? Always bearing in mind that we didn't have much. . . . I started into writing a proposal which we might propose. It called for an expedition into North Africa. . . . Just as I was finishing, King came in. It is remarkable now, but King accepted [it] without a quibble. Usually argued over all our plans.[43]

Forrest Pogue summed up the chiefs' dilemma:

> The main problem . . . between the Joint Chiefs and the President vis-à-vis the British on the matter of Mediterranean versus Cross-

Channel strategy came from the fact that Churchill realized that
Roosevelt believed it absolutely essential for American forces to be
in action in the European area in 1942. And inasmuch as the main
forces available for any operation across the Channel in that year had
to be largely British, it was quite clear that no matter how often the
British Chiefs and the Prime Minister said, "Well, we'll talk about
that," that there was not going to be any Operation Cross-Channel
that year. And that no matter how much King and Marshall opposed
the idea of a North African operation, that would probably be all
that was left that would be staged.[44]

Franklin Roosevelt later told Samuel Eliot Morison that on
August 1, 1942, when he received word that a final agreement had
been reached between the British and American staffs on the North
Africa operation, he sent a message to Winston Churchill responding "Thank God!"[45]

With Operation Torch now on, King and Marshall had to find
ways of keeping in check FDR's inclination for following Churchill
into further Mediterranean "sideshows." As Marshall later remarked,
"Roosevelt had a habit of tossing out new operations. I called it his
cigarette lighter gesture [making an expansive move of his hands as
he said it]."[46] Ernie King was equally concerned. As he told a select
group of newsmen—the so-called Arlington County Commandos—
in an off-the-record talk in November 1942, ". . . Churchill's theory
of the 'soft underbelly' of the turtle is [not] too sound. The occupation of Sicily means only that it is necessary to occupy Sardinia. After
that, a frontal attack on Italy, and when you bump against the Alps,
what have you got? You still aren't in a position to threaten Germany
directly, because the Alps block you."[47]

Although they were unable to block further Mediterranean
operations during much of 1943, Marshall and King found to their
relief that Franklin Roosevelt began reasserting his support for the
invasion of northern France—dubbed Operation Overlord—once
American military and naval forces in the European theaters began

significantly increasing in strength. Until almost 1944, though, Marshall and King could not be certain that FDR would avoid following Churchill farther into southern Europe's "soft under-belly," and they did their utmost to see that Roosevelt stuck to the American Overlord plan.[48] This brings to mind a final humorous anecdote that Forrest Pogue liked to tell about Roosevelt and the Quebec Conference in 1943. Following a first meeting at Quebec, FDR and Churchill traveled down to Hyde Park for the weekend. Marshall, who was worried that Churchill's eloquence might weaken Roosevelt's resolve for Overlord, called in General Thomas Handy. As Pogue remarked:

> So Marshall said to Handy, "Now we've got the President where he says he'll back us, but he's seen the Prime Minister, so you go down [to Hyde Park] and ride the train up [to Quebec] with him and try to get him back on the track." Well, General Handy said, "That was quite a big order. I wasn't in that exalted a position. But I got on the train and made my way back towards where the President's car was and just when I thought I was in a position perhaps to put across my argument, I stepped on Falla [sic] [FDR's scottish terrier]." So he said, "I wasn't sure whether we were gonna keep the President in line or not."[49]

Luckily for the chiefs, Roosevelt stuck to his support for Overlord despite Handy's faux pas.

Conclusions

Despite differences in personality and outlook, President Franklin Roosevelt and Admiral Ernest King developed a solid working relationship that did much to strengthen the country's war effort. Probably the most important traits that FDR brought to his role as commander in chief were his ability to pick forceful, capable military leaders and, once having decided upon the particular directions of national military strategy, to let them control military operations with a minimum of interference. It is a legacy that all too often has been honored in the breach by the presidents who have followed him.

NOTES

1. The views expressed in this paper are those of the author alone and do not necessarily represent those of the Department of the Navy or the Department of Defense.

2. Entry for August 31, 1943, Harold D. Smith Diary, Franklin D. Roosevelt Library, Hyde Park, New York; quoted in James MacGregor Burns, *Roosevelt: The Soldier Of Freedom* (New York: Harcourt Brace Jovanovich, 1970), 349.

3. Aspects of Roosevelt's personality have been revealed in any of a large number of biographies about the man. For this chapter, I have chosen to select traits discussed in Burns, *Soldier Of Freedom,* and Frank Freidel, *Franklin D. Roosevelt: A Rendezvous with Destiny* (Boston: Little, Brown and Co., 1990).

4. Burns, *Soldier Of Freedom,* 62.

5. The quote is from Robert E. Sherwood, *Roosevelt And Hopkins: An Intimate History* (New York: Harper & Brothers, 1948), 3.

6. George C. Marshall, "Interviews with Forrest C. Pogue," tape 14, February 11, 1957, in Larry I. Bland, Joellen K. Bland, and Sharon Ritenour Stevens, eds., *George C. Marshall: Interviews and Reminiscences for Forrest C. Pogue,* rev. ed. (Lexington, Va: George C. Marshall Research Foundation, 1991), 419. See also Marshall's comment on this situation in tape 9, Jan. 15, 1957; 282.

7. Forrest C. Pogue, "The Joint Chiefs of Staff in World War II," in *JCS Reorganization Conference Proceedings, 28 February 1986,* [ed. Jeffrey G. Barlow] (Fairfax, Va: National Institute For Public Policy; prepared for the Office of Naval Research, Department of the Navy, 1986), 6; author's collection.

8. Burns, *Soldier Of Freedom,* 452-53.

9. Marshall, "Interviews,'" tape 14, in Bland, Bland, and Stevens, *Marshall: Interviews and Reminiscences,* 413.

10. For brief descriptions of the effects of these treaties on the navies of the major signatory powers, see Jeffrey G. Barlow, "World War II: Allied and German Naval Strategies," and Jeffrey G. Barlow, "World War II: U.S. and Japanese Naval Strategies," in *Seapower and Strategy,* ed. Colin Gray and Roger W. Barnett (Annapolis: Naval Institute Press, 1989), 215-16, 251, 270n.

11. Enclosure (recounting a dinner party with King George VI and Prime Minister Winston Churchill) to letter from Stark to Knox, March 20, 1944, 4, folder 3, box 6, Frank Knox Papers, Operational Archives, Naval Historical Center, Washington, D.C. (hereafter OA). It should be noted, however, that Stark was inaccurate in his implied chronology. Although he implies in his comment that the final decision in favor of the 16-inch gun battleships was made by FDR in 1935, it actually occurred in 1937, during Stark's final months as chief of the Bureau of Ordnance. For documentary evidence of Roosevelt's reluctance to arm the new U.S. battleships with 16-inch guns because of naval arms control considerations, see the letter (with enclosure) from Secretary of the Navy Claude Swanson to Roosevelt, April 7, 1937, the memo from FDR to the secretary of the Navy, April 8, 1937, and the memorandum from Swanson to FDR, April 10, 1937 (all attached), in "Navy: Oct. 1936-37" folder, box 57, Departmental File: Navy, President's Secretary's File, FDR Library.

12. Memo from FDR to the secretary of the Navy, December 23, 1940, 1, "Navy: Nov.-Dec. 1940" folder, box 59, Departmental File: Navy, President's Secretary's File, FDR Library.

13. Emphasis in original. Remarks made by John McCrea to Samuel Eliot Morison, recounted in letter (carbon) from Morison to Elting Morison, Feb. 17, 1960; tipped in to rear cover of Samuel Eliot Morison's copy of Elting E. Morison's book *Turmoil and Tradition: A Study of the Life and Times of Henry L. Stimson* (Boston: Houghton Mifflin Co., 1960), author's collection.

14. The first quoted portion is from Robert William Love, Jr., "Fighting a Global War, 1941-1945," in *Peace And War: Interpretations of American Naval History, 1775-1978*, ed. Kenneth J. Hagan (Westport, Conn.: Greenwood Press, 1978), 264. The second is from Robert W. Love, Jr., "Ernest Joseph King: 26 March 1942-15 December 1945," in *The Chiefs of Naval Operations*, ed. Robert W. Love, Jr. (Annapolis: Naval Institute Press, 1980), 140.

15. Thomas B. Buell, *Master of Sea Power: A Biography of Fleet Admiral Ernest J. King* (Boston: Little, Brown and Co., 1980), 91.

16. Xerographic copy of a typed manuscript by Admiral Francis S. Low, U.S. Navy (Ret.), entitled "A Personal Narrative of my Association with Fleet Admiral Ernest J. King, U.S. Navy," 1; "LOW, FRANCIS S." folder, box 260, Individual Personnel Records section, World War II Command File, OA.

17. King, "Roosevelt: Misc. Notes," n.d. (circa 1950), King Manuscripts, Whitehill-Buell Collection, Library, U.S. Naval War College, Newport, Rhode Island; quoted in Robert W. Love, Jr., "FDR as Commander in Chief," in *Pearl Harbor Revisited*, ed. Robert W. Love, Jr. (New York: St. Martin's Press, 1995), 175.

18. President Roosevelt went on to say, "That's not *exactly* his reasoning, but it's close enough, it'll serve." Emphasis in original. Quoted in Elliott Roosevelt, *As He Saw It*, (New York: Duell, Sloan and Pearce, 1946), 82.

19. Pogue, "Joint Chiefs of Staff in World War II," 17.

20. Emphasis in original. Letter from FDR to King, August 12, 1942; "Navy: July-Dec. 1942" folder, box 59, Departmental File: Navy, President's Secretary's File, FDR Library.
21. Barlow, "Allied and German Naval Strategies," 238.
22. Memorandum from FDR to Knox, Feb. 26, 1942; Secretary of the Navy Papers, RG 80, National Archives; quoted in George H. Lobdell, "Frank Knox: 11 July 1940-28 April 1944," in *American Secretaries Of the Navy*, vol. 2, *1913-1972*, ed. Paolo E. Coletta (Annapolis: Naval Institute Press, 1980), 712.
23. Morison's notes on conversation with FDR, June 12, 1942, box 14, Samuel E. Morison Office Files, OA.
24. See, for example, Memo from Stark to FDR, August 21, 1940; "Navy: July-Oct. 1940" folder, box 58, Departmental File: Navy, President's Secretary's File, FDR Library.
25. See, for example, memo from Stark to FDR, September 4, 1939, 1-2; "Navy: Jan.-Sep. 1939" folder; memorandum from CNO to the naval district commandants, "Forces for Naval District Neutrality duties," September 18, 1939, 1, enclosure to memo from Captain D. J. Callaghan, naval aide to the president, to FDR, October 27, 1939; "Navy: Oct.-Dec. 1939" folder; and Memo from Stark to FDR, February 5, 1940, 1, "Navy: Jan.-Mar. 1940" folder, all box 58, Departmental File: Navy, President's Secretary's File, FDR Library.
26. See, for example, Robert W. Love, Jr., "Fleet Admiral Ernest J. King, United States Navy, 1878-1956," in *Men of War: Great Naval Leaders of World War II,* ed. Stephen Howarth (New York: St. Martin's Press, 1993), 89.
27. See, for example, memo "NOTES OF MEETING AT THE WHITE HOUSE WITH THE PRESIDENT AND THE BRITISH PRIME MINISTER PRESIDING," Dec. 23, 1941, 1-3; Item 8 in a folder of Arcadia-related papers; "ARCADIA PAPERS, Dec. 1941, Exec. #4, Item #13," box 22, [Army] OPD Executive Files, 1940-1945, RG 165, NA; and memo by LTG [Brigadier General Leonard T. Gerow, War Department General Staff], "Notes of a Conference held at the White House on December 26, 1941, at 3:30 p.m.," 1-2; "1941 ARCADIA - Papers Post Arcadia Collaboration, GYMNAST, Exec #4 Filed W/ Item 13" folder, same box. For an example of Admiral King's thinking on the troopship escort issue, see memorandum from King to Marshall, "Navy Escorts for Army Transports," FF1 serial 00133, Feb. 24, 1942; "King Papers, February 1942" folder, box 1, Ernest J. King Papers, OA.
28. Memo from Forrestal to the under secretary of war, Mar. 5, 1942; "King Papers, March 1942" folder, box 1, King Papers, OA. This document was originated by Vice Admiral Richard S. Edwards, COMINCH chief of staff and an old submariner.
29. See, for example, memo from Louis C. Compton, assistant secretary of the Navy to FDR, Apr. 22, 1940; "Navy: Apr. 1940" folder, box 58; and memo from Frank Knox to FDR, "Submarine Destroyer Proposed By Lt. Comdr.

A. C. Dam, USNR (Ret.)," Apr. 12, 1941 (with attachments), "Navy: Jan.-June 1941" folder, box 59, both in Departmental File: Navy, President's Secretary's File, FDR Library. See also memo from Captain John McCrea, naval aide to the president, to FDR, Jan. 17, 1942, "Navy Department: 1934-Feb. 1942" folder, box 4, Safe File, President's Secretary's file, FDR Library.

30. Letter from FDR to Andrews, June 24, 1942, 2; enclosure to memo from FDR to secretary of the Navy, June 25, 1942, folder 1, box 5, Knox Papers, OA. The president also sent a copy of this letter to Admiral King.

31. Love, "Ernest Joseph King," 154-55.

32. Letter from Parmenter to Lieutenant Commander Henry Reck, USNR, Dec. 12, 1946, 2, correspondence folder, box 12, Morison Office Files, OA.

33. Letter from Barker, deputy chief of staff, headquarters COSSAC, to Major General Thomas T. Handy, Operations Division, War Department General Staff, Nov. 17, 1943, 1, "MAJ. GEN. THOS. T HANDY SEXTANT Nov. 1943, ITEM #15, EXEC #5, (FOLDER #3)" folder, box 30, OPD Executive Files, RG 165, NA.

34. See Love, "Ernest J. King," 91. For a review of Frank Knox's changing perspective on the Battle of the Atlantic from early 1942 through mid-1943, see Jeffrey G. Barlow, "The Views of Stimson and Knox on Atlantic Strategy and Planning," in *To Die Gallantly: The Battle of the Atlantic,* ed. Timothy J. Runyan and Jan M. Copes (Boulder, Co.: Westview Press, 1994), 33-36.

35. For a detailed discussion of these plans, see Maurice Matloff and Edwin M. Snell, *Strategic Planning For Coalition Warfare 1941-1942, The United States Army In World War II, The War Department* (Washington, D.C.: Office of the Chief of Military History, Department of the Army, 1953), 177-97.

36. Message from the prime minister to the president, June 20, 1942, enclosure to memo from Captain McCrea to Marshall and King, same date; "MEMO TO THE PRESIDENT, ITEM #34 EXEC #10" folder, box 53, OPD Executive Files, RG 165, NA. For General Marshall's written response to this message, see memo from Marshall to FDR, OPD 2904, n.d., same folder. For a discussion of the earlier Gymnast ideas, see, for example, memo from Marshall to FDR, "North Africa," Dec. 26, 1941, and memo from Marshall to FDR, "North Africa," Jan. 9, 1942, both in "North Africa" folder, box 4, Safe File, President's Secretary's file, FDR Library.

37. Churchill to FDR, July 8, 1942, in Warren Kimball, ed., *Churchill and Roosevelt: The Complete Correspondence,* vol. 1 (Princeton: Princeton Univ. Press, 1984), 520.

38. Memo from Marshall and King to FDR, "Latest British Proposals relative to Bolero and Gymnast," July 10, 1942, 1, "MEMOS FOR PRESIDENT, ITEM #53 EXEC #10" folder, box 55, OPD Executive Files, RG 165, NA.

39. Quoted in Love, "Ernest Joseph King," 152. See also Buell, *Master of Sea Power,* 107.

40. Memo from Colonel John R. Deane, secretary, General Staff, to Admiral King relaying the president's telephone message, July 12, 1942, "MEMOS FOR

PRESIDENT, ITEM #53, EXEC #10" folder, box 55, OPD Executive Files, RG 165, NA.

41. Memo from Joint Chiefs of Staff to FDR, "Pacific Operations," July 12, 1942, 1, "MEMOS FOR PRESIDENT, ITEM #53, EXEC #10" folder, box 55, OPD Executive Files, RG 165, NA.

42. Matloff and Snell, *Strategic Planning*, 272. Useful documents relating to the hasty preparations for the London trip can be found in the "DIRECTIVES AND PAPERS, MARSHALL'S LONDON TRIP, ITEM #35, EXEC #10" folder, box 53, OPD Executive Files, RG 165, NA.

43. George Marshall, "Interviews," in Bland, Bland, and Stevens, *Marshall: Interviews and Reminiscences*, 580-81.

44. Pogue, "Joint Chiefs of Staff in World War II," 10.

45. Morison's notes on conversation with FDR, Dec. 16, 1942 folder, box 14, Morison Office Files, OA. Such a message, however, does not appear among the Churchill-Roosevelt correspondence files at Hyde Park or the Public Record Office at Kew (London). See Kimball, *Churchill and Roosevelt: Correspondence*, 1: 543-53.

46. George Marshall, "Interviews," in Bland, Bland, and Stevens, *Marshall: Interviews and Reminiscences*, 599.

47. Letter from Glen C. H. Perry, deputy Washington bureau chief, *New York Sun*, to Edmond P. Bartnett, managing editor, *New York Sun*, Nov. 30, 1942, in Glen C. H. Perry, *"Dear Bart": Washington Views Of World War II* (Westport, Conn.: Greenwood Press, 1982), 110.

48. Marshall remembered, "Our whole idea was to keep the president on the course he had accepted. Always worried when the prime minister got near him." George Marshall, "Interviews," in Bland, Bland, and Stevens, *Marshall: Interviews and Reminiscences*, 620.

49. Pogue, "Joint Chiefs of Staff in World War II," 12.

CONTRIBUTORS

KENNETH S. DAVIS has authored numerous works treating FDR, including *Invincible Summer: An Intimate Portrait of the Roosevelts,* and a comprehensive, four-volume biography: *FDR: The Beckoning of Destiny, 1882-1928; FDR: The New York Years, 1928-1933; FDR: The New Deal Years, 1933-1937;* and *FDR: Into the Storm, 1937-1940.*

DR. DAVID F. TRASK, former Chief Historian, U.S. Army Center of Military History, has published *Admiral William Shepherd Benson* (with Mary Klachko) and numerous other works that describe the interaction of U.S. naval, military, and civilian leaders during World War I.

DR. RONALD H. SPECTOR, the Director of Naval History from 1986 to 1989, and currently a professor at George Washington University, has written several highly regarded histories of twentieth-century naval affairs.

DR. MICHAEL A. BARNHART, Professor of History at State University of New York, Stony Brook, has, in recent work, focused on the origins of World War II in the Pacific, especially from the Japanese perspective.

DR. JONATHAN G. UTLEY, Professor Emeritus of the University of Tennessee, is the author of *Going to War with Japan, 1937-1941* and numerous book contributions and scholarly articles relating to the prelude to World War II in the Pacific.

DR. THOMAS C. HONE, currently teaching at the George C. Marshall Center for European Security Studies in Garmisch, Germany, is a recognized authority on the history of the U.S. Navy, especially during the interwar years.

DR. WALDO HEINRICHS, Professor Emeritus of San Diego State University, is the author of *Threshold of War: Franklin D. Roosevelt and American Entry into World War II,* and of numerous books, chapters, and articles on the diplomatic and military aspects of twentieth-century American involvement in Asian affairs.

DR. HAROLD D. LANGLEY, the Smithsonian Institution's former Curator of Naval History, has published histories of the U.S. Navy and *Roosevelt and Churchill: Their Secret Wartime Correspondence* (with Francis Lowenheim and Manfred Jones).

COLONEL PAUL L. MILES, USA (RET.), has taught history at the U.S. Military Academy and Princeton University, is the author of several analyses of U.S. military leadership in World War II.

COMMANDER THOMAS B. BUELL, USN (RET.), has received a number of prestigious awards for his *The Quiet Warrior: A Biography of Admiral Raymond A. Spruance* and *Master of Sea Power: A Biography of Fleet Admiral Ernest J. King.*

DR. JEFFREY G. BARLOW is a historian with the Naval Historical Center. He has published the award-winning *"Revolt of the Admirals": The Fight for Naval Aviation, 1945-1950* and numerous treatises on U.S. naval leaders and the strategic aspects of World War II.

INDEX